The Grizzlies Migrate to Memphis

The Grizzlies Migrate to Memphis

▲▲▲▲▲▲▲▲▲▲▲▲▲▲▲▲▲▲▲▲▲▲▲▲▲▲▲

FROM VANCOUVER FAILURE TO SOUTHERN SUCCESS

Łukasz Muniowski

Sport and Popular Culture   *Brian M. Ingrassia, Series Editor*

The University of Tennessee Press / Knoxville

The Sport and Popular Culture series is designed to promote critical, innovative research in the history of sport through a wide spectrum of works—monographs, edited volumes, biographies, and reprints of classics.

Library of Congress Cataloging-in-Publication Data

Names: Muniowski, Łukasz, author.
Title: The Grizzlies Migrate to Memphis : from Vancouver failure to southern success / Łukasz Muniowski.
Description: First edition. | Knoxville : The University of Tennessee Press, 2023. | Series: Sport and popular culture | Includes bibliographical references and index. | Summary: "In the 1990s, the NBA was trying to capitalize on the latter part of the Michael Jordan era and reposition the league for an international market. Expansion franchises were granted to two Canadian cities; but while Toronto thrived thanks in large part to the drafting of Vince Carter, Vancouver badly mismanaged its team, leading eventually to the team's relocation to Memphis. Author Łukasz Muniowski finds in the shifting fortunes of the Vancouver/Memphis Grizzlies a significant window on a volatile moment in NBA history. He first examines the failure, both financially and culturally, of a prosperous Canadian city to support an NBA expansion team before turning to the Grizzlies' explosive rise in a relatively impoverished southern city starving for national recognition"—Provided by publisher.
Identifiers: LCCN 2023022324 (print) | LCCN 2023022325 (ebook) | ISBN 9781621908395 (hardcover) | ISBN 9781621908401 (pdf)
Subjects: LCSH: Memphis Grizzlies (Basketball team)—History. | Vancouver Grizzlies (Basketball team)—History.
Classification: LCC GV885.52.M46 M86 2023 (print) | LCC GV885.52.M46 (ebook) | DDC 796.323/640976819—dc23/eng/20230602
LC record available at https://lccn.loc.gov/2023022324
LC ebook record available at https://lccn.loc.gov/2023022325

To Thomas and Brian, whose editing and support
guided this book to its final shape

Contents

Illustrations

Foreword

The 2010–2011 season was an epiphany for the Memphis Grizzlies and their fans. After ten years in the Bluff City, the team finally won its first playoff games and even came within one game of the Western Conference Finals. Although just a year or two earlier some pundits had predicted the team might have to move again, now it seemed like the Grizzlies—with their tough defense and gritty inside scoring game—were here to stay.

Professional sports franchises are a means of fueling urban growth, a way for civic boosters to attract tourists and, potentially, convince current and potential residents that a city will keep growing and making money. Sports, in other words, signify success. They provide symbolic value, with winning teams validating a city's seemingly never-ending competition with other urban centers. Seen in this light, the story of the Vancouver and Memphis Grizzlies is not just a simple narrative of late-twentieth-century franchise relocation, but rather it is a complex story of global capitalism and sports consumerism.

In *The Grizzlies Migrate to Memphis: From Vancouver Failure to Southern Success*, historian Łukasz Muniowski uses vivid prose and enlightening juxtapositions to expose how two North American cities hoped to profit from hoops—while also showing how the National Basketball Association, like other pro leagues before it, worked to tap into international markets.

Modern sport, as Muniowski clearly argues, can be understood as a standardized commodity: With common rules that transcend national borders, a game like basketball can (at least in theory) be played and consumed in just about any place; players and spectators can enjoy basketball in Eastern Europe roughly the same as their counterparts in North America. And by creating expansive markets transcending national boundaries, professional leagues like the NBA develop economies of scale that, ultimately, promise to turn larger profits.

In the waning years of the Cold War, Canada was a logical place for NBA expansion. As of the early 1990s, Canada had a population of more than 27 million—about ten percent fewer than California's 30 million— yet it had no NBA teams, compared to California's four teams in Los Angeles, Sacramento, and the San Francisco Bay Area. Opportunity awaited, and the idea of American sports leagues entering the Canadian market was not a novel one. Baseball's major leagues had already placed teams north of the border, with the Montreal Expos in 1969 and the Toronto Blue Jays in 1977. It was time for basketball to get on board, and the early 1990s seemed like the right time to go international. The Berlin Wall fell in 1989, the Soviet Union collapsed in 1991, America's "Dream Team" dominated the hardwood at the 1992 Barcelona Olympics, and the North American Free Trade Agreement (NAFTA) was signed just a few months after Michael Jordan wore an American flag to obscure the Reebok logo on his Olympic jersey. The Cold War was thawing, a Pax Americana was beginning, and capital was ready to flow. National borders seemed as porous as nets—as open as the hoops themselves.

Vancouver was a logical place for NBA expansion. It was a modern, energetic city with a modern arena and a history of international expositions, especially the 1986 World Exposition on Transportation and Communication, better known as Expo 86. Vancouver was ready to put itself on the global sporting map. Indeed, students of sport history may be wise to consider the pervasive links between exposition and expansion: How many times since the mid-twentieth century has a city exploited its newfound global reputation after a major fair by seeking a new team or transforming grounds or facilities into a home for a pro team? Canada's greatest Pacific Coast city seemed poised to be the next Montreal or San Antonio.

As Muniowski shows us, however, economic reality got in the way. Basketball may be a standardized commodity, but much of the NBA's labor pool is drawn from the United States, and the talent wants to be paid in US dollars, not Canadian. As exchange rates fluctuated, it was hard for Vancouver to turn a profit. The so-called "Dream City" was a successful global metropolis that exemplified the promise of New Urbanism, but it could not keep its basketball team.

The fan base was intense, but it was small, and the Grizzlies had to move.

Enter Memphis, where the Grizzlies were reborn. Oddly enough, the Bluff City had once had a basketball team by the same name, the result of a different squad that migrated from Toronto to Tennessee in the 1970s. In the early 2000s, like three decades earlier, the Grizzlies came to town because of an unusual sort of migration: not from Rust Belt to Sun Belt, but from a thriving city north of the border to a gritty town on the Mississippi River. But the second time it worked. After a few years in the United States, the franchise thrived. Muniowski clearly illustrates how the Grizzlies' newfound success was based in large part on successful drafts and personnel moves that created a "Grit and Grind" team fitting Memphis's blue-collar identity and appealing to its largely Black fan base.

The Bluff City fell in love with its new team.

The Grizzlies were not the only NBA team to relocate in the early twenty-first century. The Hornets moved from Charlotte to New Orleans in 2002 and the SuperSonics moved from Seattle to Oklahoma City in 2008. Like other migrations, the Grizzlies' story represents the shifting topographies of professional sports. Ultimately, big-time sport is entertainment, and it goes where it can be profitable (It is no wonder that as I write these words, news outlets are reporting that Las Vegas will soon be getting its third big-league team, with the impending move of baseball's Oakland Athletics sometime before the start of the 2027 season). At the turn of the millennium, a city perched on the river bluffs of West Tennessee—a city without other big-league teams in baseball, football, or hockey—was one of those places.

Memphis may be a single-franchise city, but as of the early 2020s its NBA team is a successful commodity signifying the Bluff City's persistent yet somewhat tenuous hold on big-time urban status. Modern sport is entertainment capitalism, and Memphis is a city willing to embrace it. FedEx Forum (opened 2004) is perched adjacent to Beale Street, now a place of rich cultural signifiers where tourists are sold a certain vision of the city within a type of urban space that at least resembles the place Memphis once was. And the Forum—if an impressive venue in its own right—may be just one in a sequence of seemingly disposable facilities, along with the Memphis Pyramid (1991), designed primarily not simply to host basketball games or other spectacular events, but mainly to extract capital from sports consumers.

This is a complex story as well as a compelling and uplifting one. I invite you to join Łukasz Muniowski in his detailed and entertaining chronicle of the Grizzlies' move from Vancouver to Memphis—from a failure in British Columbia to a success in Tennessee.

Brian M. Ingrassia
West Texas A&M University

A Timeline of the Vancouver/Memphis Grizzlies

09/15/1989   The construction of the Memphis Pyramid begins.

07/13/1993   Beginning of construction of the General Motors Place, which is supposed to serve as the new home for the Vancouver Canucks of the NHL. Owner Arthur Griffiths hopes that the privately funded arena will also bring an NBA franchise to the city.

04/11/1994   The NBA Board of Governors approves the decision to award an expansion franchise to Vancouver, which will be named the Vancouver Grizzlies

07/22/1994   Stu Jackson is officially named general manager of the Grizzlies.

06/28/1995   With their first ever draft pick, the Vancouver Grizzlies select Oklahoma State's Bryant Reeves, sixth overall in the 1995 NBA Draft.

11/03/1995   The Grizzlies play their first official NBA regular season game, in Portland against the Blazers.

11/05/1995   The Grizzlies play their first official NBA regular season home game in GM Place, against the Minnesota Timberwolves. They start the season 2–0, but lose the next 19 games.

06/26/1996   The Grizzlies select Shareef Abdur-Rahim with the third overall pick. He will become the franchise's best player during its Vancouver incarnation.

07/08/1997   Bryant Reeves signs a six-year/$64.5 million contract, making him the highest-earning athlete in British Columbia.

08/07/1997   The Grizzlies trade a future first-round draft pick to the Detroit Pistons for veteran power forward Otis Thorpe.

06/30/1999   The Grizzlies draft Steve Francis with the second overall pick, despite the player stating multiple times that he will not play for them.

08/28/1999   Francis is traded to the Houston Rockets

04/11/2000   Michael Heisley is approved as the new owner of the Vancouver Grizzlies, under the condition that he will go out of his way to keep the franchise in the city.

04/14/2001   The franchise plays it last home game in Vancouver and, after two away games, finishes its sixth season in the NBA with an overall record of 101 wins and 359 losses.

06/23/2001   The Grizzlies move their basketball department to Memphis. The team will play in the Pyramid until a new arena is constructed.

06/27/2001   Shareef Abdur-Rahim is traded to the Atlanta Hawks in exchange for the third overall pick in the 2001 draft, Pau Gasol.

04/24/2002   Gasol is named Rookie of the Year, becoming the first Grizzly to win an individual NBA award. In 2006, he will become the first Grizzly All-Star.

04/30/2002   Jerry West is named the Grizzlies' executive vice president of basketball operations.

06/20/2002   The construction of the FedEx Forum begins.

05/22/2003   The Grizzlies land the second overall pick in the draft lottery, only for the Pistons to claim it due to the 1997 Thorpe trade. The 2003 draft turns out to be one of the best in league history.

04/17/2004	Following the first winning season in franchise history (50–32), the Grizzlies appear in their first playoff game. Jerry West is named Executive of the Year, while head coach Hubie Brown is named Coach of the Year.
07/12/2006	After three years of first-round playoff exits, the Grizzlies decide to take a step back, and they exchange team cornerstone Shane Battier for rookie Rudy Gay.
10/02/2006	A new potential ownership group led by Duke alumni Brian Davis and Christian Laettner is presented during a press conference.
01/15/2007	Davis and Laettner fail to meet the deadline for buying the Grizzlies.
06/28/2007	With the fourth pick in the draft, the team selects point guard Mike Conley.
07/01/2007	Jerry West steps down as the general manager after his contract is up, Chris Wallace assumes the position.
02/01/2008	Pau Gasol is traded to the Lakers in exchange for three players, two first-round picks and the rights to Pau's younger brother, Marc.
06/25/2009	With the second pick in the draft, the Grizzlies select Hasheem Thabeet, who turns out to be one of the biggest draft disappointments in league history.
07/17/2009	The Grizzlies acquire Zach Randolph from the Clippers.
09/10/2009	Allen Iverson signs a one-year deal with the Grizzlies.
11/16/2009	Iverson's contract is terminated.
07/13/2010	The Grizzlies sign defensive specialist Tony Allen, and the Grit & Grind Grizzlies are soon born.
04/29/2011	In their first postseason appearance in five years, the Grizzlies eliminate the first seed in the Western Conference, the Spurs, and lose in seven games to the Thunder in the second round.

06/11/2012   Mike Heisley sells the franchise to Robert J. Pera.

05/15/2013   The Grizzlies make the Western Conference Finals.

02/07/2019   Marc Gasol, the only remaining player from the Grit & Grind era, is traded to the Toronto Raptors.

06/20/2019   The Grizzlies draft Ja Morant, number 2 overall in the NBA Draft.

12/11/2021   The Grizzlies retire Zach Randolph's number 50 jersey.

In his book on the city of Vancouver, Lance Berelowitz writes that it "has always been whatever newcomers want it to be, the perennial immigrants' city of the imagination: Dream City."[1] That was exactly what the group of prospective NBA owners hoped it would become for the league's expansion committee in 1992, when they started lobbying to establish a professional basketball franchise in Vancouver. Arthur Griffiths, the son of a local sports magnate and media mogul, became the face of the expansion process. NBA basketball was colorful, spectacular, and flashy. It seemed to bring excitement wherever it went. Having an NBA franchise would reaffirm Vancouver's reputation as Dream City. Ever since the days of the American Baskteball League (ABL) in the 1920s, professional basketball's expansion beyond the confines of the New York metropolitan area allowed far away cities to bond over a common interest in sports franchises and the challenges they faced trying to run them.

And while the ABL folded in 1931, the NBA persevered. Following the 1992 Olympics in Barcelona, and the popularity brought to the sport by the dominance of the Dream Team, the NBA became a global sensation. With interest in the NBA at an all-time high, expanding the league to Vancouver could have the same effect the major leagues had had on Southern cities in the 1960s—it would serve as proof that the city was major league as well. Ignoring the advice of his parents, who said that owning an NBA team would be too expensive and too risky, Griffiths wanted what was popular—he wanted basketball. He thought that by having two franchises in the GM Place, the arena he was building in Vancouver, he would be able to generate twice as much revenue. His

NHL team, the Vancouver Canucks, were in need of a new home, and an extra tenant in the arena would mean more events as well as additional exposure to new consumers who did not necessarily follow hockey.

Griffiths paid the $100,000 NBA application fee and only then started looking for investors willing to help him establish a basketball franchise in a city that lacked significant basketball history. The franchise was supposed to be called the Mounties, but the Royal Canadian Mounted Police objected. The unnamed franchise was in fact losing money before it had even signed its first player. The personnel decisions were rarely good, the talent not there, and team marketing almost non-existent. The Vancouver Grizzlies were always picking in the draft lottery, because they were simply bad at professional basketball. In their sixth season in the league, with relocation already inevitable, they won their 100th NBA game. Their draft picks would range from disappointing, to having weight issues, to openly rejecting the franchise and demanding a trade before even stepping foot in Vancouver. Concerned about the impact of the move on their reputation, development, and earning ability, free agents did not want to sign with the Grizzlies.

When Michael Heisley bought the franchise in 2000, NBA commissioner David Stern agreed to the deal because the Illinois-based magnate promised he would go out of his way to keep the franchise in Vancouver. A year later, he moved the Grizzlies to Memphis. Memphis seemed like the least prospective expansion destination in the 1970s, 1980s, and even 1990s for a league considered "too Black" because of "players' apathy and excessive salaries," both of which were considered African American traits by people looking for somebody to blame for the league's lack of mainstream success.[2] The NBA wanted to lure white, middle-class consumers, and a predominantly Black city was not a good marketing location, despite the league's being predominantly Black. Furthermore, Memphis had a complicated history of racial tension, as demonstrated by such events as the 1866 Memphis city riots; the lynching of Black woodcutter Ell Persons in front of ten thousand people in 1917; and the murder of Martin Luther King Jr. in 1968. The city had seen considerable success at the college level, with the University of Memphis Tigers enjoying great local support; but on the professional level, Memphis's ABA franchise was a disaster on par with what the Grizzlies had experienced in Vancouver.

And yet, after a couple of years, the Memphis Grizzlies became a perfect small-market team. They had a devoted fanbase, a blue-collar ethic, and players who were proud of being a part of the franchise. The team played boring, rough basketball . . . and the local fans loved it. The Grizzlies replaced the folk heroes of old: Larry Finch, Johnny Neumann, even Anfernee Hardaway. Hardaway's return to the city as the coach of the Tigers' NCAA team solidified him as a college star, a Memphis prodigal son whose promising professional career had been derailed by injuries. These Grizzlies were not stuck between adolescence and adulthood, they were men. Tough, ferocious, and strong. They fought tooth and nail for every ball, scrapped for every point, and worked in unison, oblivious to individual gains.

The prosperous, ethnically diverse, and close-to-nature Vancouver looked like the perfect landing spot for what the NBA was trying to become in the 1990s. The league was trying to capitalize on the popularity of the 1992 Dream Team in Barcelona by launching a global takeover, and Canada would be its first target. On the surface, it made perfect sense. Inventor of the game, James Naismith was born and came of age in Canada. Inspiration for the sport also came from three highly popular games in Canada: rugby, lacrosse, and duck on the rock.[3] In 1988, the United States took away Canada's prized possession, The Great One, after seducing him with the glitz and glamour of Hollywood. When Wayne Gretzky was traded from the Edmonton Oilers to the Los Angeles Kings, and the Canadian-born NHL franchises were relocating to the United States, it felt like a challenge was being thrown to the Canadian sports empire. If Canada would house not one but two basketball teams, and they succeeded at playing a sport associated with the inner-city, it would make for perfect revenge. The NBA wanted to prove basketball's newly won supremacy as the most popular American-born sport in the world, and Canada was the safest testing ground for it.

Just a year before the NBA was set to take the court in Toronto and Vancouver, Canadian basketball was rocked by scandal. The men's national basketball team's head coach, Ken Shields, who was white, cut two Black players, Cordell Llewellyn and Wayne Yearwood, from the 1994 national team prior to the world championships in Toronto. The athletes accused the coach of racism. The national team consisted of seven white and five Black players. Shields was unable to adapt his style to accommodate players more reliant on athleticism, performing better without the tactical constraints. It was the usual conflict around how much individualism should be allowed in a team sport such as basketball. Shields was accused of favoring white players over Black, which was basically equal to accusing him of racism. The allegations of unfair treatment came after the tournament, and an independent investigation cleared Shields of the charges. The players who made the accusations refused to take part in the investigation, and the coach left the position after the investigation was completed.

Oblivious to the scandal, the NBA went along with the move, and the Vancouver Grizzlies took court in Portland on November 3, 1995. They proved to be a scrappy bunch and triumphed over the favored Trail Blazers. The Blazers were Oregon's franchise, on a streak of 810 sellout home games, dating back to April 8, 1977. The streak would end four home games later, with the Blazers starting the season 3–6, including going 0–4 at home. The Grizzlies' front office would love to emulate the success that the Blazers enjoyed in their home state, but despite the cities being separated by only 315 miles, the fates of the two franchises could not have been more different. Despite evidently being in crisis, the Blazers would still make the playoffs for the fourteenth time in a row. The Grizzlies would win their next game, the home opener against the Timberwolves, and then go on a nineteen-game losing streak.

The NHL's Vancouver Canucks would notoriously break their fans' hearts in the postseason. The Grizzlies were so bad that the few fans they had gave up on them annually around January-February, with the team out of the playoff picture around the mid-season mark. On the whole, they would win just 22 percent of their games, and set their franchise record for regular season wins, with 23 in their final year in Vancouver, when it was already established that they were relocating to Memphis.

Out of all the places they could move to, Memphis was the most eager to take in an NBA franchise. The city was such a promising NBA destination that the Grizzlies initially had to rival the Charlotte Hornets for a chance to move to Tennessee. Hopes of bringing the best basketball league in the world to Memphis dated back to 1988, when local cotton merchant William B. Dunavant Jr. wanted to buy the San Antonio Spurs.

In the summer prior to the negotiations, the Spurs drafted 7'1" center David Robinson out of the Naval Academy. They knew that it would take him two years to get into the league, as he needed to fulfill his obligation to the Navy and serve on active duty, but that sense of obligation and responsibility was partly the reason they decided to draft him in the first place. If Dunavant decided to shell out the $50 million that Spurs majority-owner Angelo Drossos demanded, Robinson would either re-enter the draft, as he was entitled to after completing his service, or play professional basketball in Memphis. If he did so, the iconic Memphis Grizzlies' 50 jersey would be most likely associated with "The Admiral" rather than with Zach Randolph. Dunavant backed out of the move and the franchise was bought by its president, B. J. "Red" McCombs, for $47 million. The Spurs were staying in Texas.

Twenty-three years later, in 2001, Memphis got another shot at an NBA franchise. Of the prospective relocation destinations (Anaheim, Louisville, Memphis, and New Orleans), Vancouver Grizzlies' veteran Grant Long said: "They're all recycled cities. They've all had teams before and lost them. If one of them gets a team again, well, Vancouver shouldn't worry. Another NBA team will be around in a few years."[4]

This book tries to assess and put into perspective why Long was proven wrong: why the Grizzlies failed in Vancouver—and there are no talks of the league making a return there—and why they became a success in Memphis, which ended up being much more than a "recycled city."

To understand why that happened one needs to go back to the idea of organized sports and how its meanings developed through centuries. Gary Whannel summarizes these changes, succinctly describing how sport "has been part of a culture of self-development, as in Ancient Greece, a form of spectacular entertainment, as in Ancient Rome, part of a pattern of popular festivity, as in Medieval Europe, a form of moral education, as in the nineteenth-century public schools, a symbolic form of ideological contestation, as in the Cold War, and a commodified global spectacle, as in the second half of the twentieth century."[5] The rise of modern sport, so the incarnation of sport we are most familiar with and—more importantly—consume most often, "was suspiciously coterminous with that of industrial capitalism and its concomitant need to regulate large concentrations of people."[6] In *Games without Frontiers*,

Joe Kennedy describes how the standardization of soccer rules lay the groundwork for it becoming a spectator sport, one that could be understood, enjoyed, and consumed all over the world—the only criterion being that fans understand said rules. With the popularity of sports, and the cultural, financial, and social capital they brought, it was only a matter of time before businessmen seized upon these sports, seeking to gratify their own interests.[7]

Kennedy evinces an ingrained antagonism in the fan-owner relationship reminiscent of the basic Marxist understanding of capitalism, with the franchise serving as the source of identity for the fans, a sense of belonging that is part of the product the franchise is selling. The owner might be the one who owns the franchise, collects revenue, employs the front office, the coaches, and the players, but the fans feel that they truly own the team. This applies to the "real" fans who see gamedays as rituals through which they affirm their identity. Erin C. Tarver describes how "this feeling of possession, or of intense, frenzied pleasure, is one that is no doubt familiar to many devoted sports fans who have had the experience of being present at the sacred space of the home field or court."[8] Possession and identity are crucial in forging loyalty to a franchise, which is expressed by said rituals. Tarver refers to the relationship of fans to franchises as "affective attachment," which requires constant, repeated action so that fans devote their energy, time and—most importantly—money to support the objects of their devotion.[9]

The technological revolution that took place in the late twentieth and early twenty-first century, along with cultural and political processes like globalization and the end of Cold War, completely transformed fandom, making it global rather than local. Fans were no longer obliged to attend home games—let alone live in the same city as the team they supported—to consider themselves "real" and their devotion still genuine. In a sense, the Vancouver Grizzlies fell victim to the changing global landscape, despite appearing as its early beneficiaries. Conceived in the early 1990s in a new, hopeful reality, the Vancouver Grizzlies were supposed to make the most of their location and serve as proof of the triumph of capitalism; however, the sole existence of an NBA franchise was not enough to keep it in Vancouver. It needed care and attention as well.

One of the features of what sociologist Zygmunt Baumann character-izes as liquid modernity is constant change, whereby "the new 'short-term' mentality . . . came to replace the 'long-term' one."[10] The Vancouver Grizzlies lost on the court, eventually lost fan interest, which resulted in the loss of revenue, and, in consequence, the City of Vancouver lost its NBA franchise. In professional sports, the process of change is integral to the seasonality of the experience. Rosters and coaching staffs change annually, with the conclusion of a season serving as the beginning of a new one. The Grizzlies, however, managed to stay surprisingly constant, regardless of who the main players were.

From 1998 to 2001, the core of the team consisted of three young play-ers: point guard Mike Bibby, small forward Shareef Abdur-Rahim, and center Bryant Reeves. However, growing pains and injuries meant they could never reach their potential as a unit and thus bring excitement to the City of Vancouver. Following the second retirement of Michael Jordan and the 1998–99 NBA lockout, league fandom collectively declined, as fans saw both sides of the conflict—team owners and players—as entitled and spoiled. The Grizzlies had recently signed two of their promising play-ers—Reeves in 1997 and Abdur-Rahim in 1999—to large extensions, even though the team was yet to win twenty games in a season, let alone make the playoffs. They were not All-Stars, All-NBA players, or the vocal lead-ers the team was hoping for when drafting them. More importantly, they were not embedded in the local community, and the amount of money they were paid did not help endear them to the City of Vancouver.

To understand why professional basketball failed in Vancouver and succeeded in Memphis, it is necessary to not only retrace the events that led to both, step by step, but also discuss the circumstances—economic, political, and social—that preceded the Grizzlies' arrival to both cities. Therefore, the first two chapters show how the Vancouver Grizzlies came to be, with the first focusing on the history of professional basket-ball in Vancouver, prior to NBA franchises becoming such sought-after commodities, and the second on the expansion process that brought the NBA to not one, but two Canadian cities—Vancouver and Toronto. The second chapter also gets into the construction of the arena, GM Place, the staff, and the roster, as well as the first two games played by the Van-couver Grizzlies.

The next two chapters showcase the differences between the Vancouver Grizzlies and the Memphis Grizzlies by comparing two somewhat similar players and their very different fates. "Two Fifties" feature two rather big, unathletic men wearing the same number 50 jersey, Bryant Reeves and Zach Randolph. They carved out two very different identities for themselves while playing for two very different teams (but the same franchise). Reeves entered the NBA as the first lottery pick of an expansion franchise, and while initially a local darling, became emblematic of the Grizzlies' failures in Vancouver. Randolph, by comparison, was not a big-name acquisition when joining the Memphis incarnation of the Grizzlies, but he embraced the City of Memphis, and it embraced his tough, blue-collar attitude back. He was so influential in Bluff City that the Grizzlies retired his number. The next chapter of the two shows the strides that the franchise had made since 1999, when it drafted Steve Francis second overall. Francis refused to come to Vancouver and the team fell apart. When the biggest name in franchise history, Allen Iverson, arrived to Memphis ten years later, he did so as a free agent, by his own admission. Granted, he was no longer the player he was in his prime, and his untimely departure from the team could have impacted the franchise negatively, but instead it united the Grizzlies. The franchise did not lose any credibility when Iverson left, unlike when Francis ridiculed it a decade prior.

The next chapter, "The Most Hated Man in the City," traces back Michael Heisley's acquisition of the Grizzlies and his efforts—or, rather, lack thereof—to keep the franchise in Vancouver. The following chapter, "Bears in the Pyramid," looks at the history of professional basketball in Memphis up to the Grizzlies' arrival as well as Heisley's attempts to build a successful team in Memphis, while trying to gain local support. The last chapter, "Grit & Grind," highlights the conclusion of that process, when the Grizzlies finally, after fifteen years in the league, carved out a distinguishable identity, one characteristic of the region in which they played.

Shareef Abdur-Rahim was the closest thing to a superstar that the Vancouver Grizzlies ever had.

Chapter 1

Nighthawks, Kodiaks, and Other Animals

Having a major league team often serves as a validation for a city or a region. Despite limited economic benefits generated by sports franchises and their facilities, a team brings abstract and symbolic value to a region.[1] It is as if a developing city has not properly *arrived* until it has its major league team—or teams—by way of expansion or relocation. In the 1960s, sports fans experienced the first wave of the great expansion, with the professional leagues growing literally and figuratively. In the period from 1966 to 1970, the NBA ballooned from nine to sixteen teams, with the inclusion of the Buffalo Braves, the Cleveland Cavaliers, the Chicago Bulls, the Milwaukee Bucks, the Phoenix Suns, the Portland Trail Blazers, the San Diego Rockets, and the Seattle SuperSonics. Furthermore, in the 1960s, five teams changed their homes: the Lakers left Minneapolis for Los Angeles, the Warriors left Philadelphia for San Francisco, the Chicago Zephyrs became the Baltimore Bullets—and the Bulls filled the void left by the Zephyrs in the Windy City three years after the relocation, the Syracuse Nationals became the Philadelphia Sixers just a year after the Warriors left, and the St. Louis Hawks moved to Atlanta.

A decade engulfed in counterculture and rebellion, when it came to professional sports, the 1960s belonged largely to the establishment. Supported by government funding, expansion and relocation teams were supposed to distract from the wars raging outside the country as well as the constant fear of nuclear warfare, and redirect attention to tangible heroes fighting for victories against equally talented opponents. Arthur Schlesinger Jr. described the decade as a constant search for "a renewal of conviction" and "a feeling of dedication . . . as if increasing numbers of Americans were waiting for a trumpet to sound."[2]

Politicians from across the political spectrum recognized sports' unifying potential and used it to advance their own policies. Newly elected president John F. Kennedy appeared on the December 1960 cover of *Sports Illustrated* with his wife posing on a yacht. The issue also featured his article, "The Soft American," about every American's duty to stay fit and healthy.[3] By the end of the decade, during the 1968 presidential campaign, Richard Nixon appeared at the Kentucky Derby to gain the support of Southern Republicans; and during the 1970 protests against US involvement in the Cambodian campaign, he talked about sports when meeting with the protesting students, discussing their university football team instead of the issue they were standing up against.[4]

The cities upon which the honor of relocation or expansion was bestowed were never accidental, and the relocation was always either in agreement with a certain trend or a response to a certain event. Such was the case with what Pat Pickens calls "The Sun Belt Shift" in the NHL. Following the Los Angeles Kings' 1988 acquisition of Wayne Gretzky, and the exposure (and revenue) made possible thanks to the trade of the best hockey player ever to a non-hockey, big-market city, the NHL expanded into southern markets, with franchises soon appearing in Arizona, Florida, and Texas. The trade was not the sole or the main reason for the league's growth, and Pickens acknowledges that as well, stating that "jobs and people were moving out of the Northeast and Rust Belt to southern and western US markets. The NHL had to keep up."[5] Still, Gretzky became the face of this cultural shift, and the trade made for a captivating narrative, a success story of sorts that every new team owner probably dreamed of replicating, regardless of the sport.

The NBA's first wave of relocation did not have such a compelling story, or a hero who could represent the growth of America's utmost professional basketball league. In the case of the Hawks' 1968 relocation from St. Louis to Atlanta—so to Tennessee's neighboring State of Georgia—the move symbolized the city being a "growing success," placing the team arena in the center of the revitalized downtown.[6] The franchises that moved to Georgia were mostly symbols and not actual objects of sports worship, with the Hawks and the MLB's Braves owner Ted Turner handling the financial burden of keeping both franchises in the city from the 1970s onwards, as both were operating at a loss.[7] Letting go of the franchises would translate to failure for white southerners, who began defining themselves by how little the differences between themselves and the northerners were—an approach that James C. Cobb refers to as "regional anonymity."[8] If the northern cities, the New Yorks, the Bostons, and the Detroits, loved their franchises so much, there must have been something about them that southerners would find lovable as well, right? In some places, the expansion team was indeed a goal in itself, the darling of the locals, who rallied around this new, artificial creature, which they were told was now theirs to care for.

Such was the case with the Seattle SuperSonics—or, more precisely, Supersonics, as they were known until 1969, when they decided to change the spelling of their name. The Sonics were not a transplant, they were an expansion team, and for some people this made a huge difference. They were born in Seattle and were supposed to be the proud bearers of everything the city stood for. Don Richman, the Sonics general manager, said: "We believe the name expresses the feeling of the Seattle people and Seattle's present and future."[9] The Seattle SuperSonics entered the NBA before the start of the 1967–68 season, along with the San Diego Rockets. With the inclusion of both teams in the league, the regular season schedule grew from eighty-one to eighty-two games. Seattle was far from the basketball-obsessed city it eventually became, as attendance in the Seattle Center Coliseum was a modest 6,186 fans per game in the Sonics' first NBA season.

The expansion Sonics managed to win just twenty-three games in their inaugural NBA season. And as the new kids on the block, they were used by the league to further test its expansion possibilities. On February 24, 1968, they got really close to beating the eventual champions, the Boston Celtics. In a high-scoring game, they led for three quarters, but in the fourth the more experienced Celtics took over, winning the last twelve-minute section by ten points, and the whole game 141–137. The game was played in Vancouver, in Washington's neighboring province of British Columbia. It was the Sonics' second visit to Vancouver, after they played a preseason game against the St. Louis Hawks in front of a crowd of twenty-five hundred fans. Over eight thousand fans showed up for their game against the Celtics—the first official NBA game played in British Columbia.

Canada was a possible new market for the NBA, much in the way the south was the somewhat uncharted territory of professional sports. Just as the South eventually recognized that the only way of saving its uniqueness following the Civil War was to adapt and "set out to pursue commerce, industry and the almighty dollar with the same avidity and finesse as the victorious North,"[10] Canada was also going through a transitional period that began after World War II. On August 10, 1960, the parliament enacted the Canadian Bill of Rights, a document that allowed Canadians to further separate themselves from British rule. The next step was polling the citizens about a new flag, as up until that point Canada was mostly using Britain's Union Jack. From close to six thousand entries, a fifteen-member committee picked the red and white Maple Leaf. The decision was announced on February 15, 1965.[11]

Just like the American south, in the first half of the twentieth century Canada was somewhat stuck in constant transition, a state of becoming, but never actually being what it aspired to. The economic expansion of Canada went hand in hand with the physical expansion of three metropolitan regions—Montreal, Toronto, and Vancouver. Their growth came at the cost of Indigenous peoples, whose reservations were taken over by provinces and their municipalities, while the Natives themselves were removed from their home territories and replaced by transients looking for work in the revived lands.[12] As unwanted as the minorities forced out of their homes following the 1929 financial crisis, the new arrivals became homeless, reliant on government programs and posing a serious danger to municipal government's finances.[13] World War II not so much revigorated as saved the Canadian economy, and the country was prospering again, producing and exporting military equipment used on the other side of the globe. Once the 1950s came around, the country was ready to showcase its progress.

And what better way to flex the proverbial muscles than through housing an international sports competition? The 1954 British Empire and Commonwealth Games were to take place in the City of Vancouver, British Columbia. However, Canada's largest port city and center of international trade lacked a proper stadium for such an event, which was why a group, whose face was local rugby legend Jack Bain, asked the public to vote on funding the venue. After officially retiring in 1939, following a fifteen-year playing career, Bain became the coach of the Vancouver Meralomas rugby team. One of the greatest and most recognizable athletes in British Columbia history, Bain was named the chairman of Games Publicity and Promotion Committee.

The construction of Empire Stadium, as the arena was meant to be called, was put to vote on December 10, 1952. Construction was estimated to cost $1,250,000. A special committee was established to ensure that the budget would not be exceeded. The agreement to construct the 36,200–seat stadium was welcomed with great enthusiasm in the press. Jack Richards of *The Vancouver Sun* was hoping that the stadium would enable the city to secure its first professional football team.[14] *The Province* wrote enthusiastically about how the stadium was going to "put the city on the western Canadian sports map in a big way," predicting that 1953 was going to be "the biggest and best year in [the city's] history,"[15] as other local investments were supposed to take place around the same time as well.

Construction of the stadium was scheduled to begin on March 1, 1953. Already at the beginning of the "best year in history," civic officials got into an argument with the local Bureau of Economic Geology about the funding. For journalist Erwin Swangard, this was to be expected, "for one familiar with the temper of this city and its officialdom it's neither surprising nor cause for concern to hear and read about disagreement in and between committees on just about every aspect of the stadium."[16] Swangard was partially responsible for Vancouver winning the right to host the British Empire and Commonwealth Games, organizing fellow journalists as well as sports icons to generate support for Vancouver instead of Hamilton, Ontario, which initially stood the highest chance of hosting the games.[17] The architects estimated that the stadium was going to cost $1,365,000, exceeding the original projection by $115,000. The price did not include parking spaces, or anything else in the radius of over forty feet around the stadium.

Construction began on May 1, 1953, two months behind schedule. Around June, a rumor began to circulate that the arena would be called Totem Stadium, a name that one alarmed citizen, "Sylvia"—possibly sharing the sentiment of the larger population, protested, writing that the name should derive from something more "dignified" than "an interesting specimen of primitive and barbaric art."[18] While southern cities of the next decade wanted to prove to their northern counterparts that they actually belonged in the progressive, integrated America, Canada as a whole wanted to prove to the world that it was no longer a British province, but a fully formed forward-thinking country. A part of that process was leaving Canada's own racist past behind.

Historians posit that the first group of Chinese immigrants arrived in Canada in search of gold in 1858 and soon found employment in mills and factories. Around seventeen-thousand workers arrived in the years 1881–1884 to build the Canadian Pacific Railway. Just a year later, in 1885, Canada implemented a Chinese head tax on newly arrived Chinese workers. Upon its introduction, the tax was $50; in 1903, it grew to $500, to prevent more immigrants from coming into the country. Furthermore, the Chinese were not allowed to become Canadian citizens, vote, or hold land. From 1923 until 1947, when the Chinese Immigration Act was in effect, almost all immigration from China to Canada was prohibited. The Chinese diaspora lived mostly in cities, in the so-called Chinatowns; up until the late 1930s the Chinese were more or less prohibited from living anywhere else. Vancouver itself was infamous for its protests and riots against the influx of Chinese immigrants. From 1887 to 1907, the city was subjected to anti-Chinese acts of vandalism. The Chinese were, supposedly, taking jobs away from locals.

In 1947, the Chinese Immigration Act was finally repealed, for a number of reasons. For one, China was invaded by Japan in 1937, and local sympathy went to those attacked. In fact, hatred toward the Japanese contributed to the positive perception of the Chinese.[19] Following the attack on Pearl Harbor in 1941, once Canada declared war on Japan, Canada and China became unlikely allies. The fact that more than two hundred Chinese Canadians volunteered to fight for a country that so stubbornly rejected them, basically forced the Canadian government to grant, first the veterans, and eventually the rest of the Chinese Canadians, the right to vote. While in 1949 only 111 Chinese immigrants were admitted to Canada, in the next five years that number grew to around two thousand annually.[20] At least on the surface, Canada of 1954 was a land of progress.

Held the same year, the Commonwealth Games were a great success, with twenty-four countries participating in the contest. More importantly, from the perspective of the development of professional sports in British Columbia, they indeed allowed Vancouver to get its first football team. Even before it was constructed, the stadium was proclaimed the future home of the B.C. Lions. The prospect of housing a professional football team was welcomed with much enthusiasm, as fifteen thousand voters picked the name after a panel of nine judges trimmed the total number of 1,168 potential names to six: Cougars, Grizzlies, (Mountain) Lions, Loggers, Totems, and Tyees. The final choice came down to Lions and Grizzlies. The panel went with Lions. From the submissions, which included a letter justifying why a given name was picked, the panel was supposed to pick a fan who would win a plane trip to New York.[21]

Vancouver already had a rugby team as well as a hockey team, the Vancouver Canucks. The Canucks were established in 1945 and played in the Pacific Coast Hockey League, which in 1951 merged with the Western Canada Senior Hockey League to form the Western Hockey League. A football team was a different animal though, with the Lions representing the whole province of British Columbia. Furthermore, a Canadian football team was a sign of deeper integration with the southern neighbor. The same could be said of walking away from the traditional, British understanding of the word "football," replacing it with "soccer." America's game did not come easy to the Lions, who won just one game in their inaugural season in the Canadian Football League. In 1964, they would win their first Grey Cup.

In 1968, Vancouver may have been considered a potential home for a professional basketball team, but it was professional baseball that first seriously broke ground in Canada, with the Montreal Expos in 1969 and the Toronto Blue Jays in 1977. The historical significance of Montreal for American sports is not limited to the twenty-four-time Stanley Cup winners, the NHL's Montreal Canadiens. On October 23, 1945, Jackie Robinson originally signed with the Montreal Royals, the farm club of the Brooklyn Dodgers, whom he would join after one season in Canada. In his account of Robinson's first major league season, Scott Simon writes that "Montreal was simply the best big city in North America for Jackie Robinson to step into the game of organized baseball," because Robinson and his wife had not experienced a single racist incident during their stay in the city.[22]

The Expos, however, never became a baseball powerhouse and, as pointed out by Frank P. Jozsa Jr., "to remain solvent, the franchise in Montreal needed to repeatedly sell its high-priced and outstanding players to other clubs. Thus, even though it developed very good players in its farm system, the Expos lacked the financial capital and fan support to retain these athletes."[23] As for the Blue Jays, their introduction was a direct consequence of the Expos finding a home in Canada, despite early struggles regarding attendance. According to Jozsa, the belief was that the biggest metropolitan region in Canada could support another professional franchise, apart from the beloved Maple Leafs of the NHL, based on the demographics and economics of the area and the incomes of households. This prediction proved to be accurate, as 1.7 million fans attended the Blue Jays' home games in 1977 despite the team's 54–107 record in the AL West Division, and even following its last-place finishes in the 1977 through 1981 MLB seasons."[24] After the 2004 season, the Expos relocated to Washington and, as the Washington Nationals, won their first World Series in 2019. The franchise's sole success in Montreal was winning the NL East Division title during the second half of the strike-interrupted 1981 season. In comparison, the Blue Jays won two World Series in Toronto, in 1992 and 1993, the first MLB team based outside the United States to do so.

As for professional basketball, the clash between the Sonics and the Celtics was the first NBA game played in Vancouver, but not the first one played in Canada. The first ever Canadian NBA game—which was then known as the BAA, Basketball Association of America—was played on November 1, 1946, between the New York Knickerbockers and the Toronto Huskies, in Toronto, Ontario. In a move to promote the event, the organizers promised anybody over 6'8" free admission—that is, anyone taller than Toronto center George Nostrand. While the game, won by the visitors 68–66, is often used as further proof of basketball's Canadian roots—after all, the inventor of the game, James Naismith, was born in Canada—only two players on the Huskies were Canadian. They were both rookies, Gino Sovran, and Italian-born Hank Biasatti, and both appeared in a total of six BAA games. The Huskies were a rather insignificant franchise, folding after just one BAA season with a 22–38 record. During that one season, the team had four head coaches, the last of which, Robert Rolfe, was a former baseball player; after the team fell apart, he became a coach for the New York Yankees.

On November 8, 2016, when playing against the Knicks, the Raptors took the court in Huskies' jerseys to commemorate the seventieth anniversary of that inaugural game. The team debuted the jerseys seven years earlier, on December 8, 2009, in a game against the Timberwolves. The Raptors rookie, Californian DeMar DeRozan, said a couple of days earlier, when the jerseys were unveiled: "We're going back to our roots. That was a while ago, way before I was born. It's great to represent what (the city) had so long ago."[25] And while the Raptors indeed had a good chance of becoming the Huskies, as the name could serve as evidence that the team historically *belonged* in the NBA alongside American franchises, "no one could create a logo that didn't look like the Timberwolves in Minnesota."[26]

The Timberwolves joined the NBA as an expansion franchise six years before the Raptors, in 1989, and the similarities between the two logos would make it hard to distinguish between the two teams, which, in turn, would negatively influence their marketability. Just like Toronto, Minnesota could stake its claim as the cradle of professional basketball, with the Minneapolis Lakers being three-time NBA champions, before relocating to Los Angeles in 1960.[27] The Wolves however did not try to capitalize on the Lakers' Minneapolis past, while the Raptors, for numerous seasons, engaged in retro marketing, despite, as pointed out by Zach Scola and Brian S. Gordon, having no connection to the Huskies.[28] The Huskies themselves were a rather questionable source of identity, as their legacy was a single, losing NBA season, which is why, following Scola's and Gordon's reasoning, the Raptors' throwback jerseys could be treated as "faux retro," due to the lack of continuity between the Canadian franchises.

The 1968 game between the Sonics and the Celtics is not remembered as fondly as the one between the Huskies and the Knickerbockers, nor does it live on in NBA lore. After all, it was just a regular season game played in an unfamiliar arena. It would take twenty years for Vancouver to house another professional basketball game, although this one would have nothing to do with the National Basketball Association. The International Basketball Association (IBA) got its name from its willingness to include teams from other countries in the organization. Initially, the global expansion of the upstart league was supposed to begin in neighboring Canada, as it was supposed to include teams from three cities: Calgary, Toronto, and Vancouver. With the rest of American teams, the founding eleven franchises held a draft in which only players 6'4" or under were allowed to participate. Along with the size limit, the new league permitted zone defense and introduced a thirty-second shot clock. The salary cap was set at $600,000 and the ten-man rosters were supposed to play in fifty-four-game seasons. Like the ABA, which tried to differentiate itself from the NBA by introducing its own three-colored ball, the IBA planned to "use a blue ball emblazoned with a world map."[29]

Even before securing an arena or a coach, the Vancouver Nighthawks, as the team was named, had thirty-five players on their protected list, from which they were supposed to pick the final ten. The draft was territorial, with the three Canadian teams assigned a US state, apart from their home provinces, to make up for the lack of local talent from which to pick. The reason for the local selections was the league's schedule, as the games were supposed to be played during the NBA offseason, from May to September, allowing players to hold other jobs when the IBA season was over. The Nighthawks picked players from the State of Kentucky, as well as the province of British Columbia. Only four of them were Canadians: Jay Triano, Eli Pasquale, Howard Kelsey, and Paul Johansson. Pasquale, who was still representing Canada in international competitions, was employed as a public relations specialist to preserve his Olympic eligibility. The 6'1" point guard was one of the best Canadian basketball players, so he was too valuable for the national team to lose. Kelsey and Johansson were also scheduled to join the team in a year, in 1989, as they still had a chance of making the Olympic roster. Up until 1992, it was necessary for players to remain amateurs in order to participate in the Olympics.

Even though the IBA was backed by big names like Calvin Murphy (the first overall pick in the draft, selected by the unnamed Toronto team) and Bob Cousy (the league's director of basketball operations), it was hard for the newly created league to gain credibility. Don Burns, the president of the Nighthawks, was mocked by *The Province*'s sportswriter Jim Taylor for selecting the 5'4" Leroy Byrd in the IBA draft. Taylor joked that Burns picked Byrd because he thought that the "L" stood for Larry, while the player could be helpful in "locating dislodged contact lenses."[30]

Soon though Byrd endeared himself to the local community, proving to be outspoken, witty, and simply likable.

Burns and Edmund Jung, both businessmen whose offices were located in Los Angeles, were co-owners of the team. In the early months of 1988, team general manager Jerry Weber was still holding tryouts for potential players, hoping to build the strongest roster possible. Meanwhile, the team finally secured its arena, the BC Place Stadium, which, like the Empire Stadium, was built to house an important international event, intended to showcase Vancouver's status as a big-time player on the international stage. This time it was the 1986 World Exposition on Transportation and Communication, which would coincide with the city's centennial year. The theme for the Expo was "Man in Motion," but the prevailing notion was that it would bring some sort of permanence to the inhabitants of the city. Patrick Reid, commissioner general and president of the event, said: "When Expo 86 is over, there should be not only evidence of its usefulness as a means of international understanding and progress, but also of celebration, excitement, cultural exchange, urban renewal and lasting benefits to the citizens of Vancouver and B.C."[31]

Reid was an Irish-born, British war hero who chose British Columbia as his home, following visits to over fifty countries as a diplomat. He served as president of the International Bureau of Expositions in Paris from 1979 to 1983, so around the time Vancouver was awarded the honor of hosting the event. Vancouver mayor Mike Harcourt was initially concerned that if the city proceeded with the proposal and invested in the Expo, it would not be possible to build a Toyota plant or a liquefied natural gas plant, both offering instant jobs to people in the province. When it was established that the projected $60 million rapid transit system was going to be built regardless of whether the Expo would be held in Vancouver, the city showed even less interest in the event.

Eventually, after months of arguments and uncertainty, the costs were divided among the Canadian government (over $1 billion), the B.C government ($800 million). and the participants ($400 million). Expo communications president Jess Ketchum stated two years before the event even took place that it already invigorated the south shore of the city, and "for the first time in 100 years, Vancouverites can be proud of this area."[32] The sense of pride could be also derived from having their own, modern stadium, which came with a $126 million price tag. It officially opened on June 20, 1983; a day later, a crowd of 60,432 fans attended the first sporting event there, with the Vancouver Whitecaps of the North American Soccer League playing the Seattle Sounders. Three days later, the B.C Lions hosted the Calgary Stampeders. Both Vancouver teams relocated to the BC Place. After their arrival, the largely industrial area started to change, giving way to condominium towers. The stadium was estimated to be around 5 percent of the total investment, as it was accompanied by city parks, affordable housing, seawall walks, and public facilities.

The world's largest air-supported dome allowed to play outdoor and indoor games and since the IBA season was not colliding with the NASL (North American Soccer League) and the CFL (Canadian Football League) schedules, the BC Place was picked as the home arena of the Nighthawks. The PNE (Pacific National Exhibition) Agrodome, capable of housing five thousand fans, was also considered a possible basketball venue, but the steep price of $6,000 per game plus 15 percent of the gross gate made it simply too expensive for the Nighthawks to play there. When reorganized for basketball purposes, the fifty-thousand-seat BC Place had around ten thousand to eleven thousand seats available, and the costs of playing there were the same as in the Agrodome, minus the gate receipts. Rumors were spread that the admission fee would reach $24 for the most expensive seats,[33] but it was actually set at $12.50. The Nighthawks purchased their basketball floor from the Anaheim Convention Center for $15,000, to be set up at the BC Place. Shipping costs almost doubled the price; still, this was a bargain, considering that a new floor cost around $60,000, and fellow Canadian franchise Calgary 88s paid $40,000 for an old floor from Kemper Arena in Kansas City.[34]

Meanwhile, the upstart league experienced its fair share of problems just months before the season was to start. The number of teams dropped from eleven to just six, two Canadian—the Nighthawks and the Calgary 88s—and four American—the Chicago Express, the Fresno Flames, the Las Vegas Silver Streaks, and the Youngstown Pride. League management, represented by chairman of the board of the IBA Management Team Ben Hatskin and Vice President Dennis Murphy advised the teams "not to play a regular season schedule in 1988," due to "lack of proper time to develop the multitude of details needed for a successful season."[35] Both men had prior experience creating professional leagues from the ground up, as they co-founded the World Hockey Association, and Murphy also lent his hand to the founding of the American Basketball Association. The board of governors decided to go along with the season anyway, as they had already put up $130,000 in management fees and performance bonds each, and changed the league's name to avoid any sort of legal action.[36] At first they intended to call their organization the International Basketball League, but the name was too similar to the originally intended IBA, so they settled on the World Basketball League (WBL).

The Nighthawks employed Bill Westphal, older brother of former NBA player Paul Westphal to be the head coach of the team. The forty-four-year-old was an assistant coach on the San Diego Clippers in 1980–82, before they relocated to Los Angeles. He also coached at Occidental College and University of Washington. Because he was still teaching at Occidental, located in Eagle Rock, California, the first week of training camp was handled by members of the front office. All players received a basic salary of $20,000 Canadian, with incentives like games won and performance per minutes played, allowing them to make up to $33,000, not counting the playoffs. The exhibition games involved the Nighthawks playing against amateur, inexperienced teams and winning by 40, 70, or 90 points. But when they faced off against the Calgary 88s in their first official game, they lost 94–132 in front of around forty-seven hundred fans. The big-name coach did not even show up, as he was officially replaced by Mike Frink before the start of the season. Frink, former assistant at University of Washington, was already working with the team during the training camp anyway. Just like Westphal, he was the older brother of a former NBA player, Pat. Pat Frink did not have as stellar a career as Paul Westphal; he injured his ankle as a bench player for the Cincinnati Royals, and his career was over after a single season.

Although the Nighthawks lost their first two games, they were becoming somewhat popular in the city, though rather as a novelty act. Leroy Byrd, the 5'4" point guard, even got his own column in *The Province*, cleverly named "Byrd's Eye View," in which he clearly defined the bold goal for his team: "Our job is to make Vancouver a basketball town."[37] For the Nighthawks' home opener, the third game of the season, 3,250 fans showed up. The team lost again, although this time in overtime, 109–112, to the Calgary 88s. The next day, just 932 fans attended a back-to-back game against the 88s and the Nighthawks' first win, 107–104. The dip in fan interest was partially blamed on the lack of basketball roots in British Columbia.

On June 7, 1988, the league took over the team. Burns stopped paying the bills, the players and the staff were not receiving their paychecks, and in three weeks the owner quit. At that point, the team reported $500,000 in losses. League Commissioner Steve Ehrhart was optimistic about the takeover: "We've made the commitment that Vancouver will finish the season. I'm quite proud of the league. Quite frankly, I think this is our strongest moment."[38] Still, there were already talks of the franchise relocating. Following the takeover, the Nighthawks went on a nine-game losing streak. Apart from the owner, general manager Jerry Weber was gone as well. Bryan Pollard, a player who left the team in September due to payment issues, was very critical of Burns and Weber: "The way the team was run . . . was bizarre. In training camp we'd have six-hour practices. It was like something out of Mad Max—only the strong survive."[39] Pollard also spoke with compassion about Coach Fink, who, according to the player, was constantly undermined by the duo.

After the turn of the year, the Nighthawks were no more. While Ehrhart expressed hope that the team could be revived next season, the league had already secured a different franchise, in Worcester, Massachusetts, to keep the number of teams at six for the following year. The league commissioner said that he was "disappointed that local groups [in Vancouver] haven't been able to put it together."[40] A similar opinion would echo over a decade later with regard to Vancouver's first and only NBA franchise. With high-quality basketball available just a two-and-a-half hour drive away, in Seattle, there was little reason for the city to rally around a dysfunctional organization that was operated from offices located in Memphis, Tennessee.

Ehrhart became league commissioner on two conditions: that the league headquarters would be located in Memphis (so he would not have to move), despite the city not having a WBL team, and that he would be allowed to keep his position at Dunavant Enterprises, Inc., a company dealing primarily in cotton trade. Before becoming league commissioner, Ehrhart was president and general manager of the United States Football League's Memphis Showboats, a team co-owned by William Dunavant and Arkansas food manufacturing magnate Logan Young. He was also the first executive director of the United States Football League (USFL), and had fifteen years of experience working in sports administration. Ehrhart found the concept of the newly established league interesting, hoping that "This [was] going to be a very fast-paced game with no slow 7-footers coming up the court."[41] When the season concluded, that faith persevered, and just two months after the Nighthawks folded, it was announced that under 6'5" basketball would be revived in Vancouver in time for the summer.

This time the team would play in the Agrodome, and it would be named the Kodiaks. Unlike the Nighthawks, the nickname made little sense, as the Kodiak bears, also known as Alaskan brown bears, as both names indicate, live at the Kodiak Archipelago, Alaska. Nighthawks, however, live in British Columbia during the warmer months, and once it gets colder, they migrate to Latin America, traveling up to twenty-thousand miles in search for a place to spend the winter. The name was somewhat prophetic; just like nighthawks, the WBL team called Vancouver home only during the summer, making it basically impossible for it to grow local roots.

Joel Loreth, who was the "caretaker employee" of the Nighthawks when Burns and Weber left the failed investment, was employed as the general manager. During his first interview as a GM, Loreth was initially hesitant to name the team's new owners, as some still had to sign the appropriate documents. Loreth intended to bring back some of the players and Coach Frink, who was not given a fair shot to turn Vancouver into a basketball town.[42] Six days after it was first reported to the press that WBL basketball would be back in Vancouver, on March 10, 1989, Rick Smith, Deni Leonard, and R. D. Forsyth were revealed to be the team owners. The three owned Asia Pacific Forest Products, Ltd., a local log exporting company.

However, when the negotiations between Commissioner Ehrhart and the ownership group hit an impasse, presumably on the issue of indemnification against the Nighthawks debt, just ten days after the owner-ship group was officially announced, the Kodiaks became history. Still, the owners stated that they hoped to revive the project the following year. Jim Jamieson of *The Province* also refused to admit complete defeat, writing: "Professional basketball, it seems, is dead in Vancouver."[43] That small glimmer of hope held by the journalist—in one of the most opti-mistic "it seems" in the history of Canadian basketball—shared by many other locals who still held the belief that Vancouver could indeed one day become a basketball town, would soon turn into something much greater than they expected.

Chapter 2

Northward Expansion

For the NBA, the 1980s was a decade of antinomies. In the first part of the decade, it was in need of serious remodeling, with the league reporting collective losses of $13 million after the 1979–80 season. The Indiana Pacers, the Denver Nuggets, and the Detroit Pistons were supposedly for sale. A report from the 1981–82 season showed between $15 and $20 million of reported loses, with only seven of the twenty-three teams operating at a profit. The state of things was blamed on growing player salaries and teams overspending in order to remain competitive.[1]

League commissioner Larry O'Brien established a special committee to focus on the more struggling franchises, primarily the Indiana Pacers and the Cleveland Cavaliers. Some of the issues would be solved after O'Brien stepped down and league operations were taken over by David Stern, whose tenure as league commissioner began with the salary cap coming into effect prior to the 1984–85 season. The twenty-one-page document produced by the special committee not only guaranteed players 53 percent of league revenue, but also meant that teams from smaller markets could finally rival league powerhouses, as now every team was allowed to allocate only a set, equal amount of money on player salaries, and every franchise was penalized for exceeding the pay limit. Furthermore, the success of one franchise translated into more revenue for the whole league. However, teams were already finding ways around the cap, as it was clear that the balance could be achieved only with big-market franchises generating revenue for the league.

Then, there were image issues caused by heavy drug use among the players. In 1980, Utah Jazz general manager, Frank Layden, said: "There is not a team in the league you can confidently say does not have a drug problem,"[2] and called for a rehabilitation program for players. Six years later, two-time All-Star, small forward John Drew, became the first NBA player to be banned for life for violating the league's substance abuse policy. He was released by the Jazz in 1984. The suspension came when he was trying to return to the NBA. Around that time, Chicago Bulls' owner Jerry Reinsdorf wanted the league to implement an involuntary testing program, with each player getting tested three to six times a season. This was a consequence of the failure of the NBA's drug prevention program, at least according to Reinsdorf, who said: "Once a player is on drugs, what the NBA has is a decent program, but there is nothing to prevent that first offense. The best way to prevent drug use is to test players before they get in trouble."[3] The players were tested, but only for cocaine and heroin use.

As is often the case, it took an actual tragedy to spark change. On June 19, 1986, the second pick of that year's NBA Draft, Len Bias, collapsed in the University of Maryland dormitory after snorting cocaine for several hours. Just two days earlier, he had been picked by the Boston Celtics to play next to Larry Bird, Kevin McHale, and Robert Parish, spearheading the generational change of the accomplished roster. The talented player died and the consequences of his death went beyond tarnishing the NBA's reputation. Politicians used the tragedy during the campaign for the 1986 national elections, with both sides of the political spectrum promising to double down on their efforts to stop drug use in the country. As pointed out by John E. Merriam: "Bias' death posed an almost media-perfect example of the dangers of drug overdose to a successful role model. Concern for his death matched closely with the concerns national media and government leaders were seeking to present."[4]

In spite of these issues, the NBA was pushing on with its expansion plans, agreeing to expand the league to up to three teams by the end of the 1980s and holding informal presentations from potential franchises in front of commissioner David Stern and the expansion committee in New York on January 12, 1987.[5] The committee consisted of five members: team owners Herb Simon (Pacers), Charlie Thomas (Rockets), Bill Davidson (Pistons), Suns' chairman Richard Bloch, and Mavericks' vice president Norm Sonju. A total of six cities were considered as possible expansion spots. Non-existent teams from Miami and Orlando were already selling thousands of season tickets prior to the meetings in order to stand a greater chance of securing an NBA franchise. Representatives of potential franchises from Minneapolis and Charlotte also attended the meeting. The two remaining ownership hopefuls, from Santa Ana and Toronto, did not come to New York.

Santa Ana was briefly replaced by St. Petersburg, Florida, but it was rather quickly pushed out by local rivals, Orlando and Miami. This left five teams in the running, with the Miami Heat and the Orlando Magic as well as the yet unnamed team from Minneapolis as three surefire choices. The expansion north of the border was intriguing, but David Stern was not yet the proponent of NBA's global dominance. Just half a year earlier, during the NBA Draft, he muttered "America's Game" while standing at the podium announcing the selection of Lithuanian center Arvydas Sabonis by the Portland Trail Blazers. It did not matter that world class talent evaluator, Boston Celtics' Red Auerbach, claimed Sabonis was "one of the three or four best centers in the world," and taking him with the twenty-fourth overall pick was a bargain—the NBA was an American organization, intended to preserve its identity as such.[6] Sabonis represented the Soviet Union, as Lithuania was under its dominion until March 11, 1990.

Furthermore, Toronto already failed not once but twice as a basketball town. In 1982, three lawyers—Joe Bolla, Don Smith, and Albert Strauss—tried to build up local interest for a potential NBA team. In the 1970s, the Buffalo Braves played a couple of their home NBA games in the Maple Leaf Gardens, but the team was eventually moved to San Diego. Frequented by around 7,500–8,000 Torontonians, the Braves' games were not generating enough revenue to justify a relocation to Canada. In the early 1980s, the era of the league's most serious financial struggles due to image issues, the lawyers began negotiating with local investors with the hope of buying the Cleveland Cavaliers from Ted Stepien. Stepien was selling the team under the condition that he would remain the minority owner, and looked forward to the move to Toronto. Stepien was known for racially insensitive comments, like saying that the Cleveland Indians ownership was "a Jewish clique" or that the Cavaliers had "too many Blacks" on their roster.[7] The Toronto group had the support of the Metropolitan Toronto chairman Paul Godfrey, while Maple Leaf Gardens' owner Harold Ballard guaranteed that the arena would be available to the team for the rent fee of $18,000 per game.[8]

Stepien eventually failed to move the Cavaliers to Toronto but he managed to bring another professional basketball franchise to the city just in time for the 1983–84 season. He paid the $180,000 expansion fee, which was way less than the NBA would demand from Toronto. In comparison, the last NBA expansion franchise, the Dallas Mavericks, had paid $12 million to join the league in 1980. The Toronto Tornados, as the team was called, became the second Canadian franchise in the Continental Basketball Association, the first being the Alberta Dusters, operating out of Lethbridge and affiliated with the SuperSonics. The Dusters' first season, 1980–81, came when the league consisted of ten teams and was planning on expanding to twelve to sixteen teams next season.[9] The team from Alberta set the league record for futility, losing thirty-four games, and winning just six. After that one season, the Dusters were moved to Las Vegas, where they became the Silvers, and a year later they once again moved, this time to Albuquerque.

Jim Drucker, the commissioner of the CBA, described Toronto as the league's "gateway into Canada," hoping that the Tornados' success would open the doors for establishing new franchises in Calgary and Vancouver "within the next two to three years."[10] The league had relatively low operating costs, at least in comparison to the NBA, but it guaranteed income to the franchises from a national television contract and compensation paid out annually by the NBA for the rights to sign up CBA players at will, as if they were free agents. That did not do much for the sustainability of the Tornados, who were moved after two years to Pensacola, following negotiations with Boca Raton, Jacksonville, Memphis, and San Diego. In its two seasons of existence, the team reported more than $1 million in losses. In their second season, the Tornados were averaging 652 fans per game. They relocated during the season, by the end of December 1985, making use of a ten-day window between home games.

Despite the failures in establishing a basketball culture in Toronto, in 1986, Toronto Sports Enterprises posted a $100,000 bond with the NBA, hoping to give professional basketball in the city one more try. The newly formed corporation was led by William Ballard and Michael Cohl of Concert Production International, David Fingold and Robert

Cohl of Fobasco Ltd., lawyer Dusty Cohl, and legendary NBA center Wilt Chamberlain. The ownership group began collecting $100 bonds on season tickets from fans; however, that was not enough to convince the expansion committee, and with the expansion fee set at $32.5 million, it was evident that the group could not meet the NBA's conditions. Just six months earlier, the price tag was rumored to be around $25 million, but the twenty-three teams and the league made use of the fact that the groups seeking franchises in Charlotte, Miami, Minneapolis, and Orlando were "too far into it to quit," as pointed out by Orlando's Pat Williams.[11] The Toronto group focused its efforts on getting an IBA—or WBL, as the league eventually became known— franchise instead.

That attempt failed as well; but in 1993, Toronto and Vancouver emerged as the two cities standing the highest chance of becoming a part of the NBA. The United States was on the verge of economic progress, which would last until the end of the decade. The beneficiary was the private sector, which was fueling the economic growth. Part of the reason was the North American Free Trade Agreement (NAFTA), a pact establishing a free trade zone between the United States, Mexico, and Canada. Negotiations for NAFTA had begun in 1990 by the Republican George Bush administration, which "made completion of the agreement a principal aim of his last two years in the office."[12] The continued pursuit of the deal by Bill Clinton, who was sworn as president in 1993, was met with some skepticism by fellow Democrats, even though it was evident that opening new markets would allow further economic expansion. It is estimated that the economies of the three participating countries profited from the elimination of tariffs on most goods. The NBA thought that a move abroad would bring more revenue and put domestic expansion on hold. Chairman of the expansion committee, Jerry Colangelo said, "What fits [the NBA's] future is the international scene, and Canada fits that to a 'T.'"[13]

The third party involved in NAFTA, Mexico, would also earn consideration for a potential NBA franchise, however the talks never got far. The league landed a two-year deal with TV Azteca to showcase fifty regular season games, the All-Star Game, and the Finals. NBA games had been played there since 1992. The first NBA game south of the border was played between the Houston Rockets and the Dallas Mavericks. Fans were not discouraged by the $30 ticket-price, which was close to the weekly minimum wage in the country. It was believed that if the league would expand beyond the United States and Canada, that would happen at the turn of the century and the primary target would be Mexico City.[14]

Belief in the global potential of NBA basketball was strengthened by the reactions of the international crowds to the 1992 Dream Team. The first-time assembly of NBA superstars on the US national basketball team during the Summer Olympics in Barcelona sparked interest in the best basketball league in the world. As Carson Cunningham observed: "The Dream Team attracted substantial viewing interest from the widest array of nations of any team or any other event at the Barcelona Games."[15] The United States affirmed its status as a global superpower thanks to extraordinary play by Michael Jordan, Magic Johnson, Larry Bird, and others. They became the faces of globalization, earned worldwide recognizability, and were regarded as carriers of American values of freedom and individuality.

The narrative was backed by the constant increase in revenue coming from retail sales, both domestic and international. In three years, the latter grew from $29 million in the 1989–90 season to $250 million in 1992–93. The exposure provided by the Dream Team led to an almost 50 percent boost in ticket sales, which were at $128 million before the Olympics in Barcelona took place. Peter Land, the league's director of marketing communications, acknowledged that, from its inception, the NBA's marketing division's goal was to make basketball "the most popular sport in the world," and "the Dream Team certainly fast-forwarded [the NBA's] international mission."[16] Commissioner Stern was however careful about rising interest from expansion groups in Cincinnati, Memphis, Orange County, and Toronto. In November 1992, he said: "We just had an expansion. . . . We're very pragmatic on this one. Just because someone wants an NBA franchise doesn't mean it's a wise business move for the NBA to expand."[17]

Now Toronto was a shoo-in as an expansion destination, as it had been knocking on the NBA's door for over a decade. The city had a head start over other potential expansion locations after taking over the 1994 FIBA World Championship hosting duties from Belgrade, following the United Nations Security Council Resolution 757, which prohibited Yugoslavia from participating in sporting events due to civil war in the country. This was a chance for Toronto to prove that it could become a basketball town. The average attendance of 10,186 fans during group games did reflect that, even though around 3,000–5,000 fans in the arenas were Croatian and 6,000–8,000 were Greek, supporting their national teams. They represented the 60,000 Croatian and 120,000 Greek diasporas in Toronto, both hailing from basketball-obsessed countries.

The so-called Palestra Group, led by local businessman Larry Tannenbaum, applied for an NBA franchise in Toronto in October of 1992. Vancouver jumped in in April 1993, making use of the strength of the bid from Toronto. Two other offers from Ontario followed. With the Vancouver Canucks to relocate to a $100–million, twenty-thousand-seat arena in 1995, Arthur Griffiths, head of Northwest Sports Ltd., to whom the hockey franchise belonged, was looking for another tenant, preferably a basketball team, that could move in there as well. The Canucks played in the Pacific Coliseum, which was constructed for $6 million in 1968. Doug Ward of *The Vancouver Sun* pointed out that the scoreboard itself at GM Place was going to cost $7 million.[18] GM Place was the first 100 percent privately funded Canadian arena to open since Maple Leaf Gardens in 1933.

Arthur Griffiths saw bringing the NBA to the city as an opportunity to step out of his father's shadow. Frank Griffiths was a media executive who, in 1974, acquired Northwest Sports, the company that owned the Vancouver Canucks, for $8.5 million. He made the purchase, at least partially, because his wife was a hockey fan.[19] Starting off as an accountant, he built his own broadcasting company, Western International Communications, which became the largest private broadcaster in Canada. In May 1981, Arthur Griffiths was named his father's assistant at Northwest Sports. He was just twenty-four years old. One of his first tasks was negotiating with the Pacific National Exhibition, the owners of the Coliseum. Arthur Griffiths was threatening that the team would build its own arena—a vision that was dismissed as too outlandish and too expensive, until 1992, when he indeed bought five acres of land for

$14 million. A year later, construction began, even though financing for the investment has not been entirely secured.

Griffiths even paid the nonrefundable $100,000 application fee to secure a meeting with the NBA expansion committee. Once again, with no financing secured. Mike Horsey of Northwest Arena Corp. pointed out that "Toronto started the process. Vancouver and Toronto can be easily paired."[20] Initially, the NBA expansion committee did not see the possibility of putting together the two offers and was hesitant to take on two new teams simultaneously, especially from a foreign market. Colangelo was sending mixed signals; one week he would tell the press that the two Canadian teams should not bid against each other, and the next that only one team from the region would join the league.[21]

The bidding war was already in full force, while three Toronto groups were engaged in their own local warfare. The aforementioned Palestra Group, apart from Larry Tannenbaum, consisted of Toronto Blue Jays baseball team owners, Canadian Imperial Bank of Commerce, and John Labatt. Another group had the backing of Capital Canada Ltd., and its face was Magic Johnson. The third group was led by former Ontario premier David Peterson, and consisted of companies like Bitove Investments Inc., Slaight Communications, and Bank of Nova Scotia. Despite the Palestra Group being the first to submit the application, it was Peterson's group that won the unnamed Toronto-team sweepstakes. However, the real winner of the meetings in New York was the group from Vancouver. Following the presentations, Colangelo said: "We came into this thinking one team. Now two is a possibility." During the same interview, he remarked that the league did not need to expand, nor did it need franchise fees in order to remain afloat.[22]

In contrast to the $32.5 million expansion fee paid by the Heat, the Hornets, the Magic, and the Timberwolves, in 1994, the ownership groups from Toronto and Vancouver were forced to pay $125 million—which served as proof of NBA's economic growth. One of the conditions of their entry into the league was that both teams would be taken off local lotteries. The fear was that if they did, other professional franchises would be forced to follow, which would cost the Canadian government $100 million in revenue. The basketball franchise would generate around $5 million annually. Still, Stern himself warned the City of Toronto that by refusing to comply, it would not be able to secure an NBA or a rumored NFL franchise, as both leagues shared philosophies when it came to gambling.

While economically the lottery made more sense than an NBA franchise, the groups' efforts to convince the local governments otherwise were aided by a spike of teenagers' and young adults' participation in sports betting. The majority of gamblers, according to the lottery company's market research, came from the age group between eighteen and twenty-four years old, accounting for 35 percent overall of all gamblers. Tibor Barsony, executive director of the Canadian Foundation on Compulsive Gambling, voiced his concern about the issue: "It's terrible. Never have so many teenagers (been) involved in actual gambling as they are now."[23] Eventually, both sides reached a compromise, and the NBA compensated Toronto for taking its team's games off the local lottery.

Vancouver faced a similar issue with its Sports Action lottery. The Finance Minister of British Columbia, Elizabeth Cull, was not willing to lose the $1.5 million-a-year Sports Action generated in NBA game bets. One of the proposed solutions was a buyout, with the ownership group to pay $3 million in order to remove NBA games from the lottery. It was eventually agreed that the group would pay $500,000 annually for five years, with all of the money going to local health care programs and charities. With seven thousand season tickets sold, and the twenty-thousand-seat arena under construction, the team that started referring to itself as the Mounties thought it could finally look for a general manager who could assemble a proper roster and hire a head coach.

The name itself soon proved to be an issue that needed to be addressed. The original logo of the Mounties featured a uniformed Mountie from the waist-up, over the letter "M," waving a flag against a maple leaf background. The name though was soon dropped, following the opposition from the Royal Canadian Mounted Police. Another proposed name was The Force, as "Join The Force" was the slogan of the season ticket commitment campaign. Griffiths was seriously considering the name, as the Mounted Police referred to themselves as "the force," which according to him was a successful compromise.[24]

There was however little enthusiasm for the name, and the search continued. It brought a lot of frustration to Griffiths, who said: "Every time we come up with a name, there's a lawyer saying there's a trademark on it somewhere in the world."[25] Finally, after names like the Beavers, the Dragons, the Orcas, the Thunder, and around a thousand others were rejected, on the news conference on August 11, 1994, at the Museum of Anthropology at the University of British Columbia, the search was officially over. The name Grizzlies was announced. Griffiths justified the selection as follows: "The grizzly is the ultimate symbol of strength and endurance. I think we captured that in our name and our logo. The grizzly inspires respect, power and fear. Our Grizzlies will do the same."[26]

The history of the name had begun much earlier though, in June of 1941, when the Vancouver Grizzlies became the city's first American football team, which folded after just one season. Afterward, their jerseys and equipment were handed down to local junior teams.[27] The new logo for the basketball team was prepared by NBA Properties, a division of the league responsible for the Charlotte Hornets' original and the Phoenix Suns' remade logos. Upon the announcement of the franchise's name, colorway, and logo, general manager Stu Jackson, said that the name "had to reflect the powerful nature of the team, the culture, geography and heritage of Western Canada and an indigenous species. . . . Drawing our inspiration from the grizzlies on the totem poles, we decided to name our team the Vancouver Grizzlies."[28]

Former head coach of the New York Knicks and the University of Wisconsin, the thirty-eight-year-old Jackson was enthusiastic about building a franchise from the ground up. Team owner Arthur Griffiths said the decision to employ Jackson was motivated not only by his basketball acumen, but also by his ability to sell the game of basketball to the local community.[29] One of his first ideas was a series of ads created in cooperation with the local stay-at-school program. In late August, the freshly announced team logo appeared on boxes of Kellogg's Frosted Flakes across Canada. During that time, Jackson was already involved in building a database of players to pick from during next year's expansion draft, traveling from one NBA arena to the next, watching games and collecting information.

Before the start of the selection process, Jackson hired the team's first coach—Brian Winters. The Grizzlies and the Toronto Raptors found themselves interviewing the same candidates for the job, Jim Cleamons

Stu Jackson was the man tasked with constructing the roster of the Grizzlies.

and Lionel Hollins, both assistant coaches on the Bulls and the Suns, respectively, but picked neither for the job. Brendan Malone, the Pistons' longtime assistant coach, was employed by the Raptors, while the Grizzlies eventually settled on Winters, a former NBA player for the Lakers and the Bucks, whose jersey number was retired by the latter. He played under legendary coach Don Nelson, and later worked as an assistant under Pete Carril at Princeton, and Lenny Wilkens in Cleveland for seven, and Atlanta for two seasons. Schooled by three basketball greats, Winters seemed worthy of finally getting a shot as a head coach. At forty-three, he signed a three-year deal. Upon his hiring, Winters said: "I'm looking forward to the challenge of shaping an NBA franchise in a brand-new market."[30] Hired just in time for the expansion draft, Winters and Jackson would soon assemble the roster that was going to take court for the new, (hopefully) exciting Canadian team.

On November 5, 1995, the Grizzlies played their first official NBA game in Vancouver. The home debut came following a preseason in which the Grizzlies won just one of their eight games—the last one, against the Sonics, and a proper prelude that took place two days earlier, in Portland. There, the Trail Blazers proved to be truly hospitable, losing to the expansion Grizzlies 80–92 in the Canadian team's first ever regular season NBA game. The score was tied at 61 at the beginning of the fourth quarter, but then the away team went on a 12–0 scoring run. The first points in team history were scored by forward Chris King, following a turnover by point guard Rod Strickland. For the home crowd, the main attraction was the debut of Arvydas Sabonis, who at age thirty finally decided to give the NBA a try. The Lithuanian center was one of the best European players in history, but he came into the league past his prime, with a body nearly devastated by injuries. On the other side of the court, the Grizzlies had a solid big man of their own, but it was not Sabonis's fellow rookie, the sixth pick in the 1995 draft, 292-pound seven-footer Bryant Reeves. Reeves began that game on the bench.

Benoit Benjamin was also 7'0", and just like Reeves he was a highly coveted first-round pick, selected third overall ten years earlier, in the 1985 draft. One of the top prospects in the country, reportedly wanted by 350 colleges, Benjamin picked Creighton because of its head coach, Willis Reed. Reed did not have a proven record as a coach, but he was a Knicks legend, two-time NBA Champion, and the synonym of toughness. The Hall of Fame center was surprisingly loose with the young player, allowing him to miss practice and excusing him in talks with the press. It was assumed that a more strict approach would discourage Benjamin and the center would leave the program.[31] While Benjamin dominated statistically, averaging 21.5 points, 14.1 rebounds, and 5.1 blocks in his junior season, the Bluejays did not make the NCAA Tournament even once during his three years there.

His college career accurately foreshadowed the fifteen years he would spend in the NBA—the teams he was on would make the playoffs just three times. Being picked by the dysfunctional Clippers also hurt his career. In his second season in Los Angeles, the team went 12–70, which was one of the worst overall records in NBA history. Benjamin stopped going out and would leave his house only for practices and games because he was being ridiculed in public.[32] The player was immature, living lavishly, and still getting big contracts despite his well-documented status as an average NBA center. When the Grizzlies picked him 22nd in the expansion draft, after Benjamin was left unprotected by the Nets, he became the highest-paid player on the expansion team, with a salary of around $4 million—the main reason he was no longer wanted in New Jersey.

While Benjamin was picked relatively late and Reeves was the team's center of the future, it was the thirty-one-year-old veteran who was named the starter in the Grizzlies' first ever NBA game. He took court alongside power forward Kenny Gattison, small forward Chris King, shooting guard Blue Edwards, and point guard Greg Anthony. In the game against the Blazers, Benjamin was the unquestionable hero with 29 points, 13 rebounds, and three blocks. After the game, he said: "I just played. I came out and worked despite all the cynics and critics. I have rebuilt myself mentally, physically, spiritually and psychologically."[33] If there was a team on which he could rebuild himself in relative peace, it was the Grizzlies, who received little media attention in the United States.

The new franchise was projected to be the worst in the league, winning around seventeen games. The second-worst Raptors' minimum was set at twenty-one wins by the bookmakers. While it was more than certain that both teams would not significantly impact the league with their play, their jerseys undoubtedly put other teams' marketing departments on notice. Most fans got the chance to see them when both teams played their first regular season games, but the Grizzlies flaunted theirs on May 18, 1995. Since the team did not have any players to pose in the jersey, the 6'3" volleyball player Gabrielle "Gabby" Reece presented the unique colorway and design. Along with general manager Stu Jackson, she broke through the banner with the team's logo sporting the turquoise, white, and black away jersey and shorts. Apart from the color, the jersey stood out thanks to its "West Coast" trim—a Black strip with white, brown, and turquoise native-looking pattern, placed around the collar, the shoulders and the right leg. With that small detail, the Grizzlies were paying respect to the Indigenous Peoples of Canada.

The jerseys were not the only thing that made an impression on the rest of the league—the Grizzlies' defensive play did as well. The Blazers committed twenty-six turnovers. Anthony and King led the team with three steals each. The point guard also had six assists, which was below his preseason league-leading average of 7.6. The twenty-eight-year-old was picked first by the Grizzlies in the expansion draft, and second overall. He followed fellow point guard B. J. Armstrong, who refused to move to Canada and was traded to the Warriors instead. The second player picked by the Grizzlies, Rodney Dent, was selected in exchange for a second-round pick from the Magic. All in all, the Raptors and the Grizzlies picked twenty-seven players. From the thirteen selected by the Grizzlies, eight made the roster. Greg Anthony was one of them. The twelfth pick of the 1991 draft, Anthony won the NCAA Tournament with University of Nevada, Las Vegas, in 1990, playing alongside Larry Johnson and Stacey Augmon.

On the Knicks, he was the backup point guard for the first three seasons, but in his fourth, coach Pat Riley more or less shut him out. Known for playing mind games with his players, the coach grew frustrated with the team and Anthony became one of the scapegoats. In Anthony's first three season his minutes per game were ascending, but then dropped from 24.9 in 1993–94 to 15.5 in 1994–95, his career-low at the time. In *The Knicks of the Nineties*, Paul Knepper describes Anthony as a player whose "shot needed work, [who] struggled to finish around the basket, and [who] occasionally made poor decisions with the ball, but he was a relentless defender."[34] On the Knicks, Anthony shot with 40 percent accuracy and would never improve in that department, finishing his career with the same field goal percentage.

The other accomplished player selected by the Grizzlies was veteran shooting guard Byron Scott. Gary Kingston of *The Vancouver Sun* calculated that the players picked by the Grizzlies in the expansion draft collectively averaged 56.1 points per game in the 1994–95 season,[35] and Scott accounted for ten of those. Stu Jackson predicted that scoring would be an issue for the Grizzlies: "I think it's the same question that faces all expansion teams in their first year. . . . A lot of it has to do with how the players come together, a lot of it has to do with how our system is structured."[36] Scott was one of the players brought in to ensure that everybody was on the same page. The thirty-four-year-old spent eleven seasons on the team that drafted him, the Los Angeles Lakers, and won three championships alongside Magic Johnson, James Worthy, and Kareem Abdul-Jabbar. After two seasons in Indiana backing up Reggie Miller, Scott was left unprotected by the Pacers and was picked up by the Grizzlies.

Anthony and Scott both acted as true professionals and accepted the move to Canada. Both also said the right things to the press, showing great faith in the team, while curbing expectations regarding the Grizzlies' first season. Scott, whom the other players on the team referred to as "Cap" before an official team captain was even named, stated hopefully: "I think I'll get as much satisfaction starting from the ground up, watching this organization grow, than in winning a championship."[37] Anthony, who played in the 1994 NBA Finals, which his Knicks ended up losing, tried to convince his teammates: "You just have to have the mentality and philosophy that we're going to play as hard as we can and play with as much discipline and execution as possible."[38]

Anthony also showed exceptional leadership by giving his number—granted, for what Anthony referred to as a "small fee"[39]—to rookie Bryant Reeves. Anthony initially wore number 2 in his rookie year on the Knicks to honor his college coach Jerry Tarkanian, but in his second season switched to number 50. Reeves wore the same number at Oklahoma State. He had already played for the Grizzlies once during his career, as that was the name of his high school team in Oklahoma. It was not until the second year of college that he flew on a plane and during the flight he referred to the United States as a "big country," which instantly became his nickname. Reeves had the small-town mentality and everybody simply warmed to him. As pointed out by his former teammate, Sean Sutton: "People just naturally like Country. Fans like him. Coaches like him. The media like him. On top of that, he's a very good basketball player. He can make a lot of money someday. If he doesn't get hurt, he can't miss."[40] These words would turn out to be prophetic, as Reeves's development was stopped by injuries.

Reeves initially became a local darling, a sort of cult figure in Vancouver. On January 7, 1996, the Grizzlies organized a "Hair Country" promotional event, during which fans could get a flat top haircut similar to that of their starting center, and afterward were allowed to attend the game against the Clippers for free. Over two thousand fans showed up. Reeves waited fourteen games for his first NBA start, but once he got it, the spotlight—as modest as it was in Vancouver—was definitely on him. Even before the start of the season, Reeves said: "I feel comfortable with the marketing situation in Vancouver because I think I'll be able to do a good job for the team."[41]

Picking sixth, the Grizzlies were considering either him, Cherokee Parks (who was drafted twelfth by the Mavericks) or high school phenom Kevin Garnett. And while the previous teams were hesitant to take a nineteen-year-old raw but vastly talented big man from Chicago, the Toronto Raptors, picking seventh, were enthusiastic about Garnett. Isiah Thomas, the Raptors' executive said to his friend Kevin McHale, executive of the Timberwolves, who held the fifth pick: "If you don't take him, I'm definitely taking him, What you're seeing in him is all true."[42] Garnett was selected fifth, the Grizzlies landed Reeves, and the Raptors settled on the 5'10" point guard Damon Stoudamire, who would go on to be named the Rookie of the Year. Just as Reeves became the face of the Grizzlies in their first year, Stoudamire became the main attraction for the Raptors' fans.

In their second game, the Grizzlies faced the Timberwolves, who had won just twenty-one games the previous season. For the Grizzlies, that would be a respectable start of their NBA journey; but for the

Brian Winters, the first head coach of the Grizzlies, was an assistant under Lenny Wilkens, who was later passed over for the Grizzlies' job.

Timberwolves, it was proof of stagnation, as the franchise, now in its sixth NBA season, was unable to get past eleventh place in the Western Conference. In 1994, the NBA blocked their proposed move to New Orleans. The Wolves were not a big-market team, hence they were not a coveted free agent destination, therefore they had to build their roster through the draft. Picking in the lottery every year, they selected either players of questionable character (Isaiah Rider in 1993) or role players at best (Felton Spencer in 1990, Luc Longley in 1991, Christian Laettner in 1992, Donyell Marshall in 1994). In Garnett, they landed their transformative player, one that eventually elevated the franchise. The Grizzlies were hoping for the same when selecting Reeves.

In the second game of the 1995–96 season, Garnett played for eleven and Reeves for seven minutes, and they both failed to score a single basket. In order to open up more playing time for the rookie center, Jackson traded Benjamin to the Milwaukee Bucks, justifying that the player was not in the team's long-term plans anyway. Winters had some doubts regarding the decision, stating that Benjamin was not in Reeves' way minute-wise: "Well, I was starting to play [Reeves] anyway, I don't know."[43] In return, the Grizzlies got point guard Eric Murdock and center Eric Mobley. Murdock was brought in to serve as a backup for Anthony, after growing frustrated with his diminishing minutes in Milwaukee following the acquisition of Sherman Douglas by the Bucks. Benjamin finished his tenure as a Grizzly after thirteen games, in which he averaged 13.9 points and 7.9 rebounds.

The Timberwolves came out with Christian Laettner at center, and the former Duke player and the only non-NBA 1992 Dream Team member did a great job at stretching the floor, limiting Benjamin's defensive ability by luring him away from the basket. Benjamin still scored the first basket for the Grizzlies in their new arena, a close-range jumper released just in time to avoid the twenty-four-second violation. The Timberwolves closed out the first half with a 12–0 run and were leading 53–42 at halftime, but then the Grizzlies managed to tie the game, and even get a lead. With the General Motors Place at capacity, in front of 19,193 fans, Christian Laettner drained a clutch corner three to tie the game at 88. The Grizzlies then failed to score in the final possession of game, but prevailed in overtime 100–98. The game-winning shot was a buzzer-beating tip-in scored by Gattison, following a missed jumper by Scott.

When Greg Anthony crossed the half court line, fans got out of their seats, cheering on the Grizzlies. Gattison, who had suffered a spinal injury the previous season, had 13 points and 13 rebounds in the game. He had been with the Hornets ever since they joined the NBA, following three seasons in Phoenix, where he missed a year and a half with a knee injury. Playing behind Larry Johnson on the Hornets in their 1993 playoff upset of the Celtics, Gattison witnessed first-hand how an expansion team can shoot up to relevance, and was not hesitant to participate in something similar in Vancouver: "I was a part of that building process and it's a good feeling. Hopefully we can do it here in a shorter amount of time."[44]

After the game, there were reasons for optimism. The arena was packed, the players were playing hard and, more importantly, winning. Before the game started, Commissioner David Stern made a brief speech in which he stated that the NBA was a better league now that it had a team in Vancouver.

After the game, Grizzlies' assistant coach Rex Hughes jokingly screamed: "82–0! Playoffs!"[45]

The Grizzlies would lose the next nineteen games.

Chapter 3

Two Fifties

On Saturday, December 11, 2021, the Grizzlies retired their first jersey. Zach Randolph, the power forward who had spent eight seasons on the team and took the Grizzlies to the playoffs in all of them apart from the first one, saw his number 50 jersey lifted into the rafters. Most NBA expansion teams of the late 1980s seemed either hard-pressed to simply have something there—the Orlando Magic retired the number 6 jersey to honor their fans, and the Miami Heat retired Michael Jordan's number 23 jersey to honor his impact on professional basketball. Others retired jerseys to pay respect to those touched by tragedy—the Hornets retired Bobby Phills's number 13 jersey and the Timberwolves retired Malik Sealy's number 2 jersey after both players died in car accidents. Apart from the two Canadian-born teams, at that time, only the Los Angeles Clippers did not have any jerseys retired. Following December 11, only two remained.

From that moment on, no player on the Grizzlies was to wear number 50. Before Randolph's arrival, though, the team already had a player who wore that number and whose jersey should have been hanging there, reminding everyone of the team's Canadian roots. Bryant Reeves, the "original" number 50 on the Grizzlies, became emblematic of the franchise's failure in Vancouver, just as Randolph became the embodiment of its success in Memphis. Zach Randolph did not play a single NBA game in Vancouver—he entered the league just as the team relocated to Memphis, and joined the Grizzlies after they had enjoyed their first period of moderate success. When the team arrived from Vancouver twenty years earlier and played its first game in Memphis on November 1, 2001, it brought along some shameful history and a lot of baggage. A transplant from Vancouver, Canada, the Grizzlies were bad. They had no winning seasons, no playoff appearances, and no players who were capable of becoming the cornerstones of a successful franchise. Free agents such as aforementioned Bobby Phills and Malik Sealy refused to sign with the team. The two were good NBA players, but far from the superstars that an NBA franchise needed in order to consider itself relevant at the turn of the century. And yet, they snubbed the Grizzlies.

As part of the expansion agreement, for three seasons, the Grizzlies and the Raptors were not allowed to get the number one overall pick in the draft. In 1995, the Grizzlies picked Reeves. In the 1996 NBA Draft, they passed on Hall of Famers Ray Allen, Kobe Bryant, and Steve Nash in favor of forward Shareef Abdur-Rahim who was a good player and the closest thing the Grizzlies had to a superstar during their days in Vancouver. The team clearly had no chance of landing Bryant, who orchestrated a trade to the Lakers on draft day, but Steve Nash, a Canadian playing high school basketball in British Columbia, would be a good choice if the team really wanted to establish a local identity. The Grizzlies' relocation to Memphis coincided with Nash turning into a solid starter on the Dallas Mavericks. Canadian fans were commuting from British Columbia to Seattle, the nearest NBA city, whenever his Mavericks played the Sonics. Nash himself said: "Nothing makes me so proud or excited as to feel that Mavericks are B.C.'s team."[1] But B.C. had its team prior to Nash's emergence as a solid NBA player, and it lost it for numerous reasons, one of which was bad draft decisions.

The argument for Nash is valid only with the benefit of hindsight. Assistant coach Dick Davey from Santa Clara University was the only US Division I coach to actually come to Victoria and see Nash play.[2] The school would eventually retire his number 11 jersey, and he would become the first student-athlete to be honored that way; prior to the NBA Draft, however, Nash was drawing comparisons to either John Stockton or Brent Price.[3] The Grizzlies were more likely to take Nash with the 22nd pick that they also held, but there was little chance that he would still be available.

In 1997 the Grizzlies picked their point guard of the future, Antonio Daniels, with the fourth overall pick. The Grizzlies could have had Tim Thomas, Tracy McGrady, or Bobby Jackson, to name a few players who were available and would go on to have better careers than Daniels. Just a year later, they traded him to the Spurs for the 24th pick in the 1998 NBA Draft and veteran forward Carl Herrera. The rookie point guard was the designated starter but was benched midseason due to his inability to keep up with faster playmakers on both sides of the court. He even collected a couple of DNPs (Did Not Play–Coach's Decision) during the season. For a team that was not going anywhere, and the player being coached by the man who was responsible for the decision to draft him, this was really telling. Stu Jackson took over the coaching duties from Winters after 125 games, out of which the rookie coach managed to win just twenty-two.

In 1998, the Grizzlies once again picked their point guard of the future. This time it was Mike Bibby, who was selected over Antawn Jamison, Vince Carter, Dirk Nowitzki , and Paul Pierce. Bibby did not work out for the team prior to the draft and was hoping to be picked first overall by the Clippers, who chose to go with raw Nigerian center Michael Olowokandi instead. When asked about being selected by the Grizzlies, Bibby said: "That's not up to me. They drafted me so I'm here to play."[4] He would become a vital cog on a team that would be just one game away from making the 2002 NBA Finals, but it was not the Grizzlies. After three seasons, prior to the franchise's relocation, Bibby was traded along with reserve point guard Brent Price to the Sacramento Kings for Jason Williams and Nick Anderson. He became the playmaker on the best team in Kings' history.

In 1999, with the second pick in the draft, the Grizzlies selected, for the third time in a row, their point guard of the future. This time they went with Steve Francis, who was very vocal about not wanting to come to Vancouver. Adding 6'3" Francis to play alongside 6'2" Bibby made little sense if the team intended to keep both players, whereas drafting a player who made it known that he did not want to become a part of the organization did not help the Grizzlies' overall image and made it even less desirable as a free agent destination. Bibby himself wanted the Grizzlies to pick Lamar Odom, the 6'10" point forward, capable of playing all five positions, versatile and quick.

And in the 2000 NBA Draft, one of the worst in league history, they held the second pick and selected athletic power forward Stromile Swift, at a time when teams were no longer being built around power forwards who relied solely on their athletic ability. Players like Tim Duncan, Dirk Nowitzki, Kevin Garnett, and Chris Webber were physically gifted, but they also helped their teams with their mid-range game and passing. When Pau Gasol was drafted in 2001, the eventual Rookie of the Year headed from Barcelona to Memphis, not Vancouver.

The team's failure in Vancouver went beyond the basketball court, as fans simply did not embrace the Grizzlies, at least in the way those in Toronto considered the Raptors their own. This was a grassroots effort, with players going out of their way to establish a rapport with local fans. Tracy Murray, who spent just one expansion season in Toronto, recounted during an interview with CBC Radio:

> We would go all over eastern Canada, driving, and selling the game of basketball, going to do autograph sessions and take pictures and speak and all kinds of different appearances that we would do. . . . We were all over the place and you would sell the game of basketball. You go out there, you play extremely hard . . . just to gain the interest of fans all over Canada, because basketball is here and we wanted it to be here to stay.[5]

When exciting swingman Vince Carter joined the team in 1998—or 1999, to be precise, due to the lockout—the stage was set for Toronto to finally embrace its basketball franchise. The name Raptors did not point to any sort of local folklore or tradition. It was a product of the times, a nineties dinosaur craze sparked by Steven Spielberg's *Jurassic Park* (1993). The name was not derived from something local that would make the Torontonians relate to their team by sensing that it was intrinsically theirs.

The Grizzlies, on the other hand, were inherently Canadian. *The Vancouver Grizzlies*. The name immediately evoked the main characteristics of the most populous city in British Columbia—"close to nature, healthy, child-friendly, and community oriented."[6] The way the city was constructed gave birth to Vancouverism—a concept of organizing life in the city around a vibrant downtown, developed public transportation, and deep consideration of nature. The "child-oriented" argument needs some explanation, as grizzly bears are not particularly human-, let alone children-friendly. And yet the Grizzlies' mascot—a grizzly bear named Grizz—landed particularly well with the young fans, as it passed the Street's Law of Huggability. Street Characters Inc., a Calgary-based firm responsible for developing numerous mascots around the world, came up with a theory that the more fur on a mascot, the better, and Grizz was approved by test audiences.[7] Later the firm would develop the mascot for another Vancouver big-league franchise, the Canucks.

In their first years in Vancouver, the Grizzlies had a different, more approachable, and real-life mascot in Bryant "Big Country" Reeves. The Oklahoman was the first draft pick in the franchise's history and it immediately became evident that he was a unique presence on and off the court. Sometimes home fans referred to him as "Sleep Country" for his slow, lethargic play. The low-key, shy big man was not leadership material, especially considering his unwillingness to report to training camp in gameday shape. In his first three seasons, he would get into form around Christmas. The weight he was carrying around, while initially a key factor in his uniqueness and the reason for his strong interior presence, put even more wear and tear on his body, resulting in a premature end to a promising NBA career.

Reeves possessed certain qualities that could endear him to any sort of local community. Asked about his earnings, he used to say: "All these contracts blow your mind, even the $1, $2 and $3 million contracts are big for throwing a rubber ball into a metal ring."[8] However, the player was not as devoted to basketball or his teammates as a true leader should be. In comparison, Shareef Abdur-Rahim already in his second season in the league, became one of the team's three co-captains. Never the outgoing type, on the road games Reeves would spend time watching movies on his own or with teammate Brent Price. During the offseason, he would immediately leave for his hometown of Gans, Oklahoma, a single-store town inhabited by a little over two hundred people.

Still, he was oftentimes the star of the team's marketing campaigns. In the franchise's first season, Reeves's haircut was the theme of the team-organized event, which encouraged fans to get the same haircuts as their idol—the crop fade. In 1997, during KidSport Week, Reeves served as a celebrity waiter at Macaroni Grill to raise funds for and bring awareness to children's fitness. During a Vancouver All-Star golf tournament Reeves and Pete Chilcutt were the only NBA players to participate, with legends Mark Messier, Joe Sakic, and Bobby Orr representing the NHL. Reeves however left his mark on the competition, hitting a journalist in the knee with the ball.[9] He donated his autographed shoes for a fundraiser organized for the Canadian Breast Cancer Foundation.

In 1996, general manager Stu Jackson referred to Reeves as the team's "youthful foundation."[10] A year later, he extended the center to a six-year, $64.5 million deal, effective after the 1997–98 season. The contract made him the richest athlete playing in Vancouver, more than anyone on the rosters of the Canucks or the B.C Lions. Up until that point, the highest-paid athlete in the British Columbia province was Canuck Pavel Bure, who was making $5 million a year. Reeves was about to earn $7.2 million, even though he was not as revered or successful as "the Russian Rocket," who made Hockey Hall of Fame in 2012. Reeves's contract rubbed many people in the city the wrong way. Herb Capozzi, the general manager who led the Lions to their first Grey Cup in 1964, said that during his time "you could have bought the whole NFL for that . . . and you could have had the entire CFL for that first million," while John McKeachie of *The Province* estimated that for the money he was about to earn, "Big Country could wolf down 29,347,826 Big Macs. Then he could wash 'em all down with 73,739,495 Big Gulps from the nearest 7-Eleven."[11]

From being selected by the Grizzlies and appreciated by the Vancouverites for his modesty to showing up at the 1999 camp out of shape, Reeves turned from local darling to laughingstock who was not traded only because nobody wanted to buy him. Things got to the point that he was booed during Fan Appreciation Night the same year. While the size of the salary may have gone against Reeves's previous statements, had he shown effort and passion, he would at least have remained liked in Vancouver. Already in the 1997–98 season, the team's first under coach, Brian Hill, who in 1995 managed to take the Orlando Magic to the NBA Finals, Reeves was criticized after his lackluster performances during the first half of the season, only to record his best streak to date following the All-Star break, when he averaged 21.7 points and 8.6 rebounds per game.

Bryant Reeves was the first player ever drafted by the Vancouver Grizzlies.

And then, suddenly, there was no basketball to be played.

The 1998–99 lockout was the third in three years, with the 1995 lockout being resolved in two months and the 1996 lockout lasting for three hours. On March 23, 1998, team owners voted 27–2 to reopen the collective bargaining agreement once the season was over. They wanted to impose limits on maximum player salaries after Kevin Garnett signed a six-year contract for $126 million with the Timberwolves, setting a precedent and serving as a measuring stick for talented, promising, yet somewhat unproven players. While Garnett's enormous contract is often cited as the crucial deal that made players demand larger contracts, it was not the only one responsible for the spike in salaries. Damon Stoudamire said that he had a different deal in mind when negotiating his own contract: "I looked at Big Country's contract. . . . I'm looking at that contract and I'm thinking, 'I don't know what I'm going to get, but I'm going to get something.'"[12]

With contracts rising so rapidly, players were earning more than ever before, but franchises were reporting losses and, according to the owners and league executives, that model was simply unsustainable. Players, who were the ones generating the profits for the league with their play, refused to give ground. So there were cancellations. First it was training camps, then exhibition games, then the first month, two, three . . . On December 8, the All-Star Game was canceled. On January 4, league commissioner David Stern openly talked about using replacement players. Twenty-nine hours before the owners were to vote on canceling the rest of the season, on the 191st day of the lockout, the sides came to an agreement. On January 6, 1999, after three months of missed games, players not getting paid and banned from team facilities, the prevailing feeling was relief. Many players thought that the season was not going to happen and did not care about staying in shape. All in all everybody lost on the lockout—players lost a part of their earnings, and fans considered both groups, players and owners, spoiled and entitled.

Reeves was the player that the Grizzlies' staff was most concerned about—as far as gameday form was concerned. With the player usually needing around three months to get into shape, a shortened camp, and a fifty-game season brought about concerns that Reeves was in for the worst season of his career. When asked by reporters after his arrival to team facilities how much he weighed, Reeves responded: "Honestly, I don't know," adding that he followed the workout schedule provided by the team trainer on his Oklahoma ranch.[13] For Reeves, the main issue was motivation: "When the lockout was on, I was able to stay motivated until sometime in November, then it kind of got a little hard to get up because it was looking more and more like there wasn't going to even be a season."[14]

Reeves's teammate, Doug West, acquired from the Timberwolves in February 1998, criticized the center's conditioning on media day, held at the beginning of training camp. During the same press conference, he also mocked the team's free agent signing and his former teammate, power forward Cherokee Parks, and demanded a trade. Upon arrival, Reeves exceeded his playing weight by fifteen to thirty pounds—the team never released the actual figure—and was immediately assigned extra pre- and post-practice training sessions. Even though he was defending his form prior to the camp, the center had to admit: "I'm not in the kind of shape I would like to be in."[15] With the perception of NBA players heavily impacted by the lockout, showing up to camp unfit and delivering such vague statements made fans and the press completely turn on "Big Country," who was now called either "Bigger Country," "Pig Country," or "Big Continent." With the ascension of the 1997 draft pick, Shareef Abdur-Rahim, and the player extending his contract with the team, Reeves became somewhat expendable—to the point that, a month into the season, Stu Jackson was looking for offers for the center, but none came. West was not traded either and stayed with the team for two more seasons, while dealing with depression and alcohol dependency.

Reeves found himself coming off the bench in the first nine games of the 1998–99 season. The center handled the demotion without as much anger as was expected from a multi-millionaire who failed at his job. The fact that he was not suspended or fined for being out of shape also did not go without notice.[16] Because of his setback, the whole offensive strategy had to be reworked. In the first half of the season, the Grizzlies won just five of their first twenty-five games. Just as the team seemed to be onto something offensively, following a three-game stretch in which Reeves averaged 19.7 points and 10.3 rebounds, he started experiencing soreness in his right knee and eventually had to undergo surgery. The Grizzlies were not going anywhere anyway.

In the next season, the NBA introduced defensive rules that would hamper Reeves's role on the court. To make basketball more attractive, it became illegal for defenders to initiate physical contact, while the shot clock after an offensive rebound was sped up from 24 to 14 seconds. With the league average of points per game in 1998–99 dropping to its lowest since the introduction of the shot clock in the 1954–55 season, and the NBA still unable to recover image-wise from the lockout fiasco, enforcing a faster pace was seen as a way out of the crisis. This was the first in a number of rule changes which would shift the spotlight from interior-dominant big men to fast, explosive guards. With Shaquille O'Neal and Tim Duncan still at the top of their powers, it would take the coaches and the players a couple of years to make use of the changes.

The rules allowed guards to either shoot more from long distance or drive to the basket, while big men were no longer essential in teams' offensive schemes. Reeves, who was not a great rebounder, shot-blocker, or overall defender, seemed now even less worthy of the big contract extension, unable to fulfill the roles expected of less-athletic big men such as himself. While, for the next two seasons, he remained a starter, his playing time decreased to 25 minutes per game, he scored in single digits, and was among the worst starting big men in rebounds (5.8) and blocks (0.6) per game. The twenty-seven- started suffering from back spasms, which kept him out of games. Things got so bad, he could barely get out of bed and his back needed to be operated on. His contract included an incentive allowing the Grizzlies to pay the player 80 percent of the deal if he missed forty-one games in a row.

During the final game in Vancouver, Reeves said: "I'm proud to be the only one left here, knowing I did help us get off to the start. I know I was part of it. Winning is not the only thing. There have been years here where I've had a lot of fun."[17] While he did move with the team to Memphis, Reeves would not appear in an NBA game again, and his contract would stay on the team's books until the summer of 2003, impacting the salary cap and making the Grizzlies pay the luxury tax. Upon his 2002 retirement, he was the franchise's record holder for games played, with 395. Following retirement, he moved back to Gans permanently to work as a cattle farmer.

The next player to wear the number 50 jersey for the Grizzlies, Zach Randolph, would become a local icon, deeply ingrained in the Memphis community. Randolph grew up in a blue-collar factory city of Marion, Indiana. His biological father went to prison when he was in grade school. He and his three siblings were raised by his mother and her boyfriend. Randolph said of his upbringing: "I grew up the hard way, but you learn how to handle adversity."[18] Some of the adversity was self-generated. As a teenager, Randolph had various issues with the law and spent some time in juvenile detention. His basketball talent however was undeniable, and he proved that on the national stage during the 2000 McDonald's All-American Game, where after a 23-point and 15-rebound performance "Z-Bo" was selected the game's MVP. He played college ball at Michigan State and after just one season declared for the NBA Draft. His coach, Tom Izzo, stressed the importance of the environment for a player like Randolph, stating that he might one day be great, but "you've just got to get him around good people."[19]

For the first six years of his career, Randolph would play for the Blazers, then spend one and a half seasons on the Knicks, and then join the Grizzlies after half a season with the Clippers, who got rid of him to make room for the number one overall pick, power forward Blake Griffin. None of the three franchises was a paragon of stability and the twenty-seven-year-old was arriving in Memphis with considerable baggage. He was universally liked, but due to off-the-court mistakes was seen as problematic. The nineteenth pick in the 2001 draft was brought onto a Blazers team which was filled with strong personalities, prone to errors in judgment, which Randolph was supposed to divert from. Playing behind Rasheed Wallace and Shawn Kemp as the third power forward in the rotation, in his first season he was not as engaged in practice as he should have been. Thirty-three-year-old Kemp was dealing with weight and substance abuse issues, while Wallace was one year removed from establishing the NBA regular season technical fouls record with forty-one. Neither was exactly role model material for the nineteen-year-old.

With two weeks left in the 2002–03 season, Randolph got into a fight with teammate Ruben Patterson. Standing up for his friend and teammate, Qyntel Woods, whom Patterson was giving a hard time to during a workout, Randolph got into a scuffle with Patterson, knocking out the fellow forward with a sucker punch. He was fined $100,000 and suspended for two games. A year later, in April 2004—the same month Randolph collected the award for NBA's Most Improved Player, following a 20.1 point- and 10.5 rebound-season, his third on the Blazers and first as a starter—Randolph's younger brother, Roger, faced criminal charges for shooting three men in a nightclub in Anderson, Indiana. Roger Randolph was part of his brother's entourage that night, and the player was rumored to be involved in the incident as well. A year later, Roger Randolph pleaded guilty to two counts of criminal recklessness and was sentenced to three years. On June 16, 2018, he was killed in a bar in Marion, Indiana.

At various points in his Blazers' career, Zach Randolph was also accused of underage drinking, street racing, and sexual assault. In December 2006, he was suspended one game and fined $133,333 for an obscene gesture shown to the Pacers fans after fouling out. In 2007, he was involved in two strip club incidents. He was granted bereavement leave to attend the funeral of his girlfriend's cousin, and in the meantime went to a strip club. The information got out to the public only because he left the establishment without paying the bill. Later on he and Darius Miles, then on the Blazers, were in the parking lot of a strip club when somebody fired shots. In the summer of 2007, Portland was openly shopping him, and the aforementioned events were more than enough to paint Randolph as a troublesome individual, maybe not even worth trading for. Frank Isola referred to Randolph as a "no-brainer" and called his group of friends "Sopranos in high-tops."[20] His averages of 20.2 points and 9.6 rebounds in his four seasons as a starter as well as the fact that he was just twenty-five years old were enough for teams to consider trading for him.

The Blazers held the first overall pick in the 2007 draft and picked center Greg Oden, around whom they wanted to restructure their roster. They picked the prototypical big man directly over Kevin Durant and Al Horford as well as future Grizzlies Mike Conley (4th overall) and Marc Gasol (48th overall, but would join the team a year later). They also unloaded Randolph to the Knicks, one of the few NBA franchises that was, at the time, even more dysfunctional than the Blazers. In exchange for Randolph and two other players, the Knicks gave away Steve Francis and Channing Frye. Francis's two-year contract was immediately bought out, and the thirty-year-old signed a two-year deal with the Rockets. After appearing in just ten games, he had to undergo season-ending surgery and would be forced to retire a year later.

The Knicks were trying to turn the page after the dismantling of the roster that made the 1999 NBA Finals. General manager Scott Layden was fired at the end of 2003, following a four-year tenure, which involved trading bad contracts for worse deals. Isiah Thomas, who took over the team after Layden, traded for even bigger contracts and overpaid for players who did not deserve such deals. In a piece written for *The New York Times* by Howard Beck, when the Knicks were 42–36 under Thomas, the Pistons' legend was quoted saying: "We have assets, we have draft picks, we've got young players and we're playing pretty good basketball."[21] Once the 2004–05 season concluded, he signed coach Larry Brown to a five-year contract worth $50 million, making him the highest-paid coach in the league, only to fire him after one season. Thomas himself took over as head coach in 2006, and the Knicks indeed won ten more games under Thomas than the season before with Brown; but thirty-three wins were not enough to make the playoffs.

Randolph joined a Knicks team led by two undersized, shoot-first guards, Stephon Marbury and Jamal Crawford, with a promising frontcourt of Quentin Richardson, David Lee, and Eddy Curry. Curry, just twenty-five years old, was entering his seventh season in the NBA. Two years earlier, Thomas signed him to a six-year, $60 million contract. Curry was coming off a career year, and sports commentators, such as *Newsday*'s Ken Berger, were putting him in the same sentence as the best centers in the league, Shaquille O'Neal and Dwight Howard, even hinting at a potential big man rivalry between the latter and Curry.[22] The center, however, suffered a shoulder injury before the start of the 2007–08 season, and a series of further injuries would hamper his development, forcing Randolph to play more at center in his first year in New York.

Randolph was frustrated with playing for the Knicks, and admitted that at times he was wondering why the team even traded for him.[23] The tensions on the team were brewing as early as November, when Stephon

Marbury, the team's highest-paid player, was taken out of the starting lineup and fined $195,000 for missing a game following the death of his aunt, even though he believed that he had Thomas's permission. The team claimed that Marbury left because he was previously taken out of the starting lineup. In December 2007, Marbury's father died and, in January 2008, after playing in twenty-four games, he underwent season-ending surgery. The tensions between the coach and the point guard spilled onto the whole franchise. Teammate Jamal Crawford complained to the press that a franchise from such a big market received so much coverage that the inner-team turmoil simply escalated the problems in the locker room: "It's been a lot, definitely been a lot of things. But who would have known if it had not gotten out?"[24]

Randolph was also affected by the situation in and around the team. When he was ejected from a game against the Kings on January 2, 2008, he threw his headband, which was a punishable offense, and he was suspended for one game. The Knicks were 8–22 at the time, their fifth loss in a row. They would endure seven series of five losses or more during the season. After a 23–59 season Thomas was replaced with Donnie Walsh in the front office and Mike D'Antoni on the bench. Walsh was tasked with creating cap space necessary to sign either LeBron James, Dwyane Wade, or Chris Bosh—one of the three superstars, who would become free agents after the regular season. On November 21, he traded away Crawford and Randolph, freeing up $27.4 million for the 2010 free agency, taking back players whose contracts were up at the end of the season.

Both players were shipped to California, Crawford to the Golden State Warriors, Zach Randolph to the Los Angeles Clippers, at the time dubbed by *The Los Angeles Times's* Mark Heisler, "the NBA's most intriguing 2–11 team."[25] The Clippers were another badly run franchise, their status as perennial failures all the more amplified by the success of their cross-town neighbors, the Lakers. There, Randolph earned another suspension, this time for punching Louis Amundson of the Phoenix Suns during a February game. He would play up to his standards, averaging 20.9 points and 9.4 rebounds, but these turned out to be empty calories on a team that won just nineteen games during the

2008–09 season. The Clippers were awarded the first overall pick in the draft, and with power forward Blake Griffin as the surefire choice, Randolph was on the outs.

The Clippers traded him to the Grizzlies for Quentin Richardson, who was in the midst of his own personal odyssey, as he changed teams four times during the summer of 2009 without playing a single game. First the Knicks traded him to the Grizzlies for Darko Milicic' four weeks later, he was on the Clippers, who traded him to the Timberwolves. After being released by them, he signed with the Miami Heat. The Grizzlies were entering their third season under executive Chris Wallace and were continuing to rebuild. The starting five of the future was: Mike Conley, O. J. Mayo (both 21 years old), Rudy Gay (22 years old), Marc Gasol (24 years old), and Hasheem Thabeet (21 years old). The young core was supposed to study under Zach Randolph and Allen Iverson, whose fallout with the Detroit Pistons heavily impacted his value on the free agent market. Both players were preceded by their reputations as troublemakers, and both spoke about playing for the Grizzlies as their chance at redemption.

Iverson appeared in three games, on November 7, took a leave of absence, and ten days later parted ways with the Grizzlies "because of personal matters."[26] The ten-time All-Star did not mesh particularly well with the team, and his refusal to come off the bench was proof that he was not willing to sacrifice his personal achievements for team success. While prior to the season he was campaigning to be the team captain, it was the other new arrival, Zach Randolph, who proved more worthy of a leadership role. In the preseason press conference, he said he was "willing to do whatever it takes. Sacrifices are going to have to be made and I'm willing to do that."[27] Randolph and Iverson were among four players on the roster who had more than three years of NBA experience; and, with Iverson gone, Randolph was tasked with being the role model for this young squad.

The Grizzlies opened the season 1–8. Then, however, something clicked, and the younger players followed Randolph's lead. That season the power forward became the second player in team history to make the All-Star Game, after Pau Gasol in 2006. With the 40–42 overall record, the Grizzlies barely missed the playoffs, but lay the foundation for seven straight playoff appearances. The next season, the team improved to 46–36, Randolph made the All-NBA Third Team. Gradually, the city rallied behind that team, and Randolph as its best player. He already felt the organization's support in May 2010, when he was accused of two separate offenses: running a drug ring in Indianapolis and being involved in a fight in a Los Angeles nightclub. General manager Chris Wallace said in a statement that "unless some other information surfaces, Zach remains a valued member of the Grizzlies family and Memphis community."[28] None did, and Randolph responded by leading the team to a surprising playoff run, as the eight-seed Grizzlies eliminated the San Antonio Spurs. It is hard to pinpoint the exact moment when Memphis fell in love with its professional basketball team, but it was somewhere during this series that the fans who were yet to witness a single playoff win showed how much they cared for their Grizzlies.

Ron Higgins of *The Commercial Appeal* wrote that "fans just wanted to see a team that played hard every night and won more often than not."[29] The sense of collectiveness, sacrifice, and hard work is what made this Grizzlies team so special. Even without starting small forward Rudy Gay, who dislocated his left shoulder in the second quarter of a February game against the Sixers and was inactive for the rest of the season (and postseason), they were able to challenge the Spurs, who just went 61–21 during the season. The FedExForum was not one of the loudest arenas in the league, and being third from the bottom in attendance was a huge reason for that. Even reaching the playoffs did not initially inspire fan support.

The inexperienced Grizzlies won the first game in Texas 101–98, after the Spurs missed their attempt at a game-tying three-pointer. The second game was equally as tied and hard fought, but the Spurs had Manu Ginobili back, who missed the first contest, and his 17-point effort led the Spurs to a 93–87 victory. In the first half of game three, Randolph had already eclipsed his 11-point effort from game two. More importantly, though, with the first postseason three-pointer of his career, he set the score at 91–86. The Spurs managed to score only two more points and lost to the Grizzlies. Game four was an easy win for the home team, which took the 3–1 lead over the Spurs after a 104–86 victory. In game five, the Spurs managed to fight off elimination thanks to a buzzer-beating miracle shot by Gary Neal, which took the game to overtime. Game six, played in Memphis, was another tied game. With less than five minutes left, and the Spurs leading 80–79, Randolph took over, scoring 10 of the Grizzlies' final 14 points. After the game, coach Lionel Hollins said: "From a pick-me-up perspective, we just got on his back, and we rode him like he was an English warhorse. He was really carrying us, we were just hanging on."[30]

In the Western Conference Semifinals, the Grizzlies played the NBA's team of the future, the promising Oklahoma City Thunder. The Thunder, just like the Grizzlies, were a transplant, relocated from futuristic Seattle to the Southwest in 2008. Two years prior, the Sonics were bought by an ownership group from Oklahoma, following the failed attempt to buy the Hornets, who moved temporarily to Oklahoma in 2005–06 because of Hurricane Katrina. The City of Oklahoma embraced the Hornets, as proven by attendance numbers. The Hornets were eleventh in the league in the 2005–06 season, as opposed to the thirtieth spot the season prior. The Sonics were acquired by an ownership group led by corporate booster Clay Bennett, who after two years moved the franchise to Oklahoma City. Just like Heisley, Bennett spoke publicly about keeping the Sonics in Seattle, while the ownership group continued to work behind the scenes to move the franchise to Oklahoma.[31] Just like the Grizzlies, the Thunder were to be the sole professional sports franchise in the city.

With the teams tied 1–1, the series went to Memphis, where it found itself overshadowed by an actual crisis. The level of water of the Mississippi River was constantly rising throughout its basin due to major storms and the springtime snowmelt. On May 11, with the series tied 2–2, the Grizzlies lost to the Thunder. Just a day earlier, the river reached its highest level, 48.03 feet, a bit under the 1937-set record of 48.7 feet.[32] Predictions underestimated the size of the water level by around three feet, but because the authorities knew beforehand about the impending flood, policemen went door to door, urging citizens to evacuate as emergency workers handed out fliers that read, "Evacuate!!! Your property is in danger right now." The notes were distributed to around 950 households in Memphis.[33] That number would later rise to 1,300 homes, and police continued to patrol abandoned buildings to prevent looting. Around 370 people moved to shelters.[34]

In three shelters in Shelby County, the team organized special free-of-charge viewings of the games, with a local company providing projectors, screens, and audio equipment. Greg Campbell, president of business operations for the Grizzlies and FedExForum, said: "We hope that our game viewings provide a welcome distraction from the current crisis and allow those displaced to remain part of the Playoff excitement despite the circumstances."[35] The games resumed as planned, with the sellout crowd rooting for the Grizzlies. Before game seven, the mayor of Vancouver placed the team's success with the community in historical context: "The city got knocked down in 1968. It got knocked down in 2003 when Hurricane Elvis hit. This flood has knocked us down. Nobody called a foul each of those times. The game kept moving. We get back up and we keep grinding and grinding and grinding. Our Grizzlies, the way they get knocked down, get up and keep playing, reminds us right now we need to keep grinding."[36] The Grizzlies were eliminated, but the team became the darling of the local community, and it almost immediately began reciprocating that devotion.

In July 2011, the Grizzlies Foundation found itself among the top-four world charities nominated for the global Beyond Sport award, alongside Liverpool FC, Manchester City, and the Philadelphia Eagles. The nomination came for the foundation's TEAM UP youth-mentoring initiative, finding mentors for various Memphis-based programs.[37] While during the Beyond Sport Summit in December the Eagles emerged as victors, the fact that a small-market team beat out better-known sports franchises from all over the world was a sign of the team's growing recognition. In August, Rudy Gay and Zach Randolph donated autographed basketballs for an auction in support of a public library. In November, stars LeBron James and Kevin Durant participated in a charity game organized by Gay and his Flight 22 Foundation. With the 2011 lockout in place, the game took place in DeSoto Civic Center, since the FedExForum was off limits. Chris Peck of *The Commercial Appeal* was lamenting the lockout's negative impact on local fandom, adding that "the Grizzlies are more than a sports franchise. They are an economic development tool, especially when it comes to recruiting businesses."[38] The Grizzlies, however, went out of their way to keep the local momentum going.

On Valentine's Day 2012, Randolph and Tony Allen hosted a party for fourteen women and twenty kids from the Memphis Family Shelter. Randolph came to the party with his six-year-old daughter. A year later, he distributed food baskets for 450 needy families for Thanksgiving, and in 2014 helped around one hundred households pay for their utilities. As kind and approachable as he was off the court, during games he earned a reputation as a bully due to his forceful and seemingly unathletic "old school" game. He would get to the basket with a series of bumps, face-ups, jab steps, pivots, and fakes, and if that failed, Randolph would shoot from mid-range or long distance. Some fans referred to his offensive rebounds as Z-Bounds, because they were so specific of him: instead of jumping over other, stronger players, he would use his body weight to keep them on the court and reach over their heads for the ball.

He would also tangle with opposing power forwards, most notably the Clippers' superstar Blake Griffin, whom he regularly took to the floor and hurled expletives at. Fittingly, "Whoop That Trick" from the 2005 movie *Hustle & Flow*, which took place in Memphis, became the team anthem. With the snippet from the movie presenting the (fictional) process of the creation of the song playing on the jumbotron, the FedExForum was busting with noise, as fans waived yellow team rally towels and chanted the song's hypnotic chorus. Randolph and Tony Allen were the two players responsible for the music selection in the locker room and they mostly played hip-hop. Rap is where Randolph got his persona from. Tzwi Tversky from hip-hop magazine *XXL* even said to the player: "You kind of carry yourself more like a rapper than a player. You keep yourself true and don't sanitize yourself for the media."[39] The tribute video during Randolph's retirement ceremony was voiced by prominent rapper Ice Cube.

Randolph spent eight seasons on the Grizzlies, averaging 16.8 points and 10.2 rebounds per game, while "Big Country" averaged 12.5 points and 6.9 rebounds during his six seasons in Vancouver. Both were big men, both wore number 50 jerseys, and both became local darlings. While Reeves eventually lost that status—a simple cattle rancher from

Oklahoma was not a good fit for a progressive, forward-thinking com-munity—and it is up for debate whether he even wanted that sort of reverence—Randolph's blue-collar work ethic, his affinity for the local music scene, and ability to feel at home in various circumstances, with different groups, turned him into a local hero in Memphis. When his jersey was retired, it was equally for what he symbolized and how he played. The Grizzlies had a talented team in 2003–2006, as well as a potential franchise player in Pau Gasol, but the city truly embraced the franchise only after Randolph's arrival.

Chapter 4

The Franchise and the Answer

All of this could have been avoided had Steve Francis followed through with his original plan and stayed in Maryland for another year. However, the 6'3" point guard decided that one season on the Terrapins was enough and declared himself for the 1999 NBA Draft. Staying in college made little sense for the talented Francis, who described his four years before entering the draft as follows: "My mother had passed away. My father was in a federal penitentiary. We had 18 people living in one apartment. I had dropped out of high school. No scholarships. No GED. No nothing."[1] Prior to Maryland, Francis enlisted at San Jacinto College in Texas as a last resort, and after a year, as a junior, moved on to a bigger and better program. A year later, he was projected to be in the top five of the NBA Draft. He originally wanted to go to Georgetown, but coach John Thompson, who ran the program, reportedly said to him: "Steve, we like you. We do. But I just had Allen Iverson. I can't have you right after Allen. I just can't have it, Steve. I'll have a heart attack."[2]

Iverson, like Francis, was not a pure point guard, but rather an undersized shooting guard. He also enjoyed the best years of his professional basketball career on the first NBA team he played for (although for a much shorter period). Both wore number 3 jerseys in the pros and both were faces of the league around the same time. Unlike Iverson, Francis did not make the Hall of Fame, but both were expected to have greater team success. What is most important for this book: both failed as Vancouver/Memphis Grizzlies. While it would be a stretch to state, as half-jokingly written by *The Commercial Appeal*'s Ronald Tillery, that "the Griz wouldn't have moved to Memphis had Francis played in

Vancouver,"[3] his impact on the fate of the franchise was much larger than Iverson's.

Francis was drafted second overall in 1999 by the Vancouver-based franchise and left before playing a single game, after a trade demand. Iverson joined the Grizzlies following a failed episode on the Pistons, which ended with the player being shut out by the team. Iverson was the biggest name to join the Grizzlies in free agency. While he was way past his prime, the signing signified the change that occurred after the relocation. Through these two players, I will show how the Grizzlies' move from progressive Vancouver, part of "Hollywood North," to a city known for barbeque and blues positively impacted the franchise and its chances of bringing in free agents.

In the 1999 draft lottery, the Grizzlies had, for the first time, the chance to land the first overall pick. With the three-year ban on number one selections enforced by the expansion deal now lifted, the Grizzlies were hoping that finally luck would come their way. A year earlier, the Grizzlies got the first pick, but due to the rule still being in effect, they had to give it up to the Clippers. In 1999, the first pick went to the Bulls, who pressed the reset button on their basketball dynasty, which set the standard for future teams to follow and would soon become the measuring stick for other championship teams. After just one losing season, the franchise got the first pick, to which Grizzlies' coach Brian Hill said jokingly: "It's a conspiracy. They just want to make the Bulls good again. NBC's orchestrating the whole thing."[4] GM Stu Jackson implied that the Grizzlies would rather use that pick in a trade that would bring in an interior defender who could also score. The draft had players like that, including the interior-dominant Elton Brand, point forward Lamar Odom, and undersized but explosive Shawn Marion. The Grizzlies however needed somebody who the team could bring in to have immediate impact on their play.

The power forward position was by far the hardest to fill in the Vancouver Grizzlies' short history. In their first season in the NBA, Ashraf Amaya, Anthony Avent, and Kenny Gattison played in the starting lineup as number fours. Next season, the main power forward was twenty-second pick Roy Rogers. In 1997–98, the starter was thirty-four-year-old Otis Thorpe. None of these players stayed on the Grizzlies longer than one season. Thorpe joined the team in exchange for a conditional first-round pick with the Detroit Pistons. The pick was supposed to be used by the Pistons between the years 1998 and 2003 with numbers two to 18. Detroit would execute that option in the 2003 NBA Draft, where they got the second pick. In a draft that brought LeBron James, Dwyane Wade, Chris Bosh, and Carmelo Anthony to the league, they selected Serbian big man Darko Milicic.

Getting Thorpe was a bargain at the time, as the Pistons were shedding cap space and getting rid of a player so in conflict with head coach Doug Collins, that whenever he was going to be put back in the game, the decision was communicated to him via an assistant coach. On the Grizzlies, he was supposed to serve as a mentor, given that he was a veteran, a former All-Star, and an NBA Champion. When NBA rookie Antonio Daniels asked Thorpe, the *de facto* rookie on the team, to help him carry the older players' bags, the power forward responded: "How about I just be the supervisor of the rookies, so I'll tell you guys what to carry."[5]

Rogers was supposed to serve as the backup to Thorpe, and he was happy with his role, adding, "It's going to take more than Otis for us to be successful."[6] After a 30-point loss in the preseason, Rogers questioned his teammates' commitment and was traded a week later. Following the move to Celtics for Tony Massenburg, Rogers was elated to play for his favorite team, but spoke fondly of the fans in Vancouver who supported the Grizzlies as they were involved in a fifteen-game losing streak, and described potentially reaching the playoffs with other Vancouver players as a "fairly tale ending."[7]

Before the season, Thorpe was seen as the missing piece of the puzzle, a big man who did not need the ball on offense and could spread the floor, while being the team's defensive anchor. Thorpe immediately made it known that he did not want to play in Vancouver. Jackson knew that the player would need some convincing, and while the Grizzlies got off to a promising 6–7 start, once the first crisis happened, Thorpe started criticizing the organization and Coach Hill, and there was just no chance he would stay in Vancouver for the whole season, let alone the second year of his contract. The Grizzlies traded him midseason to the Kings for power forward Michael Smith and point guard Bobby Hurley.

Hurley was waived after the season, which was a disappointing end to a disappointing, injury-filled professional career of a great college player. Smith was the starter after Thorpe was traded, but after the summer and the lockout, he lost the starting job to free agent acquisition Cherokee Parks, whom the Grizzlies considered making their first ever draft pick instead of Bryant Reeves back in 1995. Parks was most known for his unconventional upbringing and his tattoos, which were widely discussed by the press in Vancouver, even though he did not have that many of them, nor were they particularly controversial. As much as the ornaments on his body, his weight was a topic of discussion, as Parks was thin and in need of putting on pounds. Parks would indeed start forty-one games of the forty-eight in which he appeared during the lockout-shortened season, but he was on the bench during crucial minutes of games.

Among the rumored trade targets for the number two pick in the 1999 draft were the Blazers' power forward Rasheed Wallace, Orlando's point guard Anfernee Hardaway, and shooting guard Nick Anderson. Hardaway would be a great addition to the postrelocation Grizzlies, as he was the product of Memphis basketball. Anderson would actually end his NBA career on the Memphis Grizzlies in 2002, a shell of his former self. The Grizzlies were also trying to get Miami's P. J. Brown for their pick as well as Dale or Antonio Davis from Indiana. Antonio Davis would end up on the Raptors and contribute to the team's success, and Dale Davis would reach the 2000 NBA Finals with the Pacers before going to Blazers.

In the meantime, the Raptors were supposedly trying to trade up in the draft in order to get Francis, who was also rumored to be at the top of the list for the Bulls and the Hornets, who held the third pick. The Raptors had number five and number twelve picks, but nothing came of the deal. The Grizzlies were not discouraged when Francis did not come to work out for them, but made them come to Maryland instead. Jackson, always the optimist, said: "He just said he wouldn't go visit the Canadian teams . . . at least we're going to be able to go and work him out."[8]

Unlike Francis, Lamar Odom wanted to play in Vancouver. So much so, that he had his first workout for the Grizzlies, knew about the strengths and weaknesses of the best players on the team when examined by the press, and said that he would be a perfect fit next to Bibby, Abdur-Rahim, and Reeves. Jackson, however, said that Odom was "the type of player that stirs the drink, he's not necessarily the main course,"[9] suggesting that taking Odom with the second pick was hard to validate. The Chicago Bulls were turned down in their attempts to trade down in the draft for a pick and either Michael Olowokandi (from the Clippers) or Tracy McGrady (from the Raptors). The Hornets wanted to pick Baron Davis third overall, despite the player not willing to work out for them either. With Francis openly dismissing the possibility of going to Vancouver, the Grizzlies went along with the selection anyway and picked the twenty-two-year-old.

When his name was called on draft night, Steve Francis was sitting with his hands folded and his head resting on the table. He needed a moment to collect himself, and once he got up, there was no smile on his face. While his family was celebrating and he entered the stage with his hands raised, the smile was still missing. Grizzlies' general manager tried to be optimistic: "He didn't appear he was the happiest guy in the draft. This is something we've faced in the past. You learn you have to deal with it."[10] With that approach, Jackson was not endearing himself to other players he was willing to bring in to Vancouver. The 1998–99 season was barely saved, the players were not exactly on good terms with team owners. And here was Jackson, forcing a kid from Maryland to move to a foreign country, even though Francis made it clear that he was not willing to play for the worst team in the league. The GM was enforcing the rules, which were still in effect, but their unfairness was becoming evident to more and more people around the league. Francis later said that he was angry about not being selected first, adding that the Bulls "took a big gamble by not picking [him]."[11] He said that signing with the Grizzlies would be a gamble as well, as he had never been to the City of Vancouver, even though that was by his own admission.

In the following month, Francis learned that he was not welcome in Canada anyway. Dan Barnes of the *Edmonton Journal* wrote that Francis was a "pouting soon-to-be-rich-kid who insulted the city of Vancouver nanoseconds after being drafted by the Grizzlies and still has not really apologized."[12] Jackson made it look as if he was hurt, stating, "We want to hand him $9 million (over three years) and make him a very well-known basketball player," and the local press was on his side, acting as if the whole country had been scorned.[13] Gary Mason of *The Vancouver Sun* wrote that by trading Francis, Jackson would set dangerous precedent by moving a player who did not want to stay in Vancouver, and others would soon follow. He also expressed regret that "the city's raw, physical beauty might attract tourists, but doesn't draw the world's best professional athletes."[14] Francis, without the Grizzlies' knowledge, intended to organize a press conference in his hometown of Takoma Park, Maryland. Information about the conference leaked on Wednesday, the conference itself was supposed to take place on Friday, August 17. A day after the announcement, Francis was traded to the Houston Rockets.

Last time a prospect taken this high in the draft held out on the team that drafted him was in 1989, when Duke power forward Danny Ferry was taken second overall by the Clippers. The other Los Angeles NBA team—sometimes affectionately called "the Anti-Lakers"—selected Ferry even though the player did not work out for the team. The Clippers already had four players on Ferry's position, including Danny Manning, whom they picked first overall a year earlier. Instead of signing with the Clippers—whose last winning season was their first in San Diego, following relocation from Buffalo, way back in 1978–79—Ferry moved to Italy, where for one season he played for Messagero Roma. In November 1989, his draft rights were traded to the Cleveland Cavaliers.

When Ferry snubbed the Clippers, beat writers were getting out of their way to ridicule team management. Mike Downey of *The Los Angeles Times* wrote that "even for the Clippers, this was something approaching a new low."[15] Tony Kornheiser of *The Washington Post* was supportive of Ferry's decision and, as validation, quoted an unnamed NBA executive, who said: "No one in his right mind wants anything to do with the Clippers."[16] Tom Sorensen of *The Charlotte Observer* described the Clippers as the league's laughingstock, and Ferry as a "fine young Duke man."[17] There were no voices in support of the Clippers, while the Canadian sports columnists felt offended by Francis's decision not to sign with the Grizzlies. No NBA franchise had ever amassed a worse four-season record than the Vancouver Grizzlies, and the men responsible for the roster decisions were still running the team. Joining the Grizzlies would simply be a bad basketball decision.

Steve Francis forced a move to the Rockets without playing a single game for the Grizzlies.

There was however something more at play here, the classist, if not racist perception of white Ferry as a respectable basketball player, as opposed to the African American "thug." His father was Bob Ferry, the general manager of the Washington Bullets, and the power forward attended Duke, whose basketball team soon became associated—albeit unfairly—with white privilege. Ten years later, in 1999, Steve Francis's refusal to sign with the team that drafted him was described by *The Vancouver Sun*'s Gary Mason as a sign that he lacked character. The same went for Francis's decision not to sign a three-year deal worth $9 million.[18] A day earlier Mason, wrote mockingly that among Francis's reasons not to come to Vancouver were: "I'll miss Grandma," and "My homies don't want to go there."[19] Tony Gallagher of *The Province* went even further, calling Francis "a stupid, ignorant dork," "an uneducated doofus," and asking: "where do the Grizzlies find people this stupid?"[20] He also referred to Francis as "kid" numerous times throughout his column. So much for known Canadian politeness.

When seventeen-year-old Francis lost his mother to cancer, he stopped playing basketball for a while. He was raised by his grandmother, whereas his "homies" were his support system. Ascribing his unwillingness to come to Vancouver to his lack of education was simply disappointing. The trade with Houston involved three teams—the Grizzlies, the Rockets, and the Magic—eleven players and three future draft picks. The most important player the Grizzlies received was Michael Dickerson, the fourteenth pick of the 1998 NBA Draft and, more importantly, Bibby's teammate on the Arizona Wildcats. The two had won the 1997 NCAA Championship together as the starting backcourt. The Grizzlies also got power forward Othella Harrington, who was backing up Charles Barkley on the Rockets for three seasons.

Both Dickerson and Harrington would enjoy the best years of their careers in Vancouver, while Francis would appear in three All-Star Games, and become one of the most popular players in the league. In 2007, following stays in Orlando and New York, he was part of the trade package that brought Zach Randolph to the Knicks. The Blazers bought out the two years remaining on his contract. At the time, Francis's career was derailed by injuries, and after signing with the Rockets in free agency, he appeared in only ten games during the 2007–08 season. On December 24,

2008, while still under contract with the Rockets and without appearing on the court that season, he was traded to the Grizzlies, now residing in Memphis, with cash considerations and the 2009 second-round draft pick that originally belonged to them, for a conditional second-round pick in 2011. Francis passed his physical and was to join the team, but was released a month later without suiting up for the Grizzlies.

He would not reach his full potential, which was initially estimated to be similar to that of Allen Iverson, however A.I. proved to be a generational talent and a culture changer for the whole NBA. Despite being generously listed at 6'0", he could score against much larger opponents. He led the league in scoring four times, made eleven All-Star Teams, and in 2001 was named league MVP. More importantly, Jeffrey Lane positions Iverson at the forefront of the NBA's hip-hop revolution: "Iverson was unabashedly proud of his ghetto roots; he bore an unpolished look plainly derived from the streets and from jail culture, had the credentials of teen incarceration, and raised unsettling concerns that he had stymied his social and basketball maturation by leaving Georgetown early."[21]

Just four months after releasing Francis, the Grizzlies were engaged in talks with Iverson, who was in the twilight of his career. After appearing in three games for the Nuggets at the beginning of the 2008–09 season, he was traded to the Pistons, who acquired him because of his expiring contract and the possibility of creating cap space in the 2009 offseason. He still made the 2009 All-Star Team off reputation rather than pure play. He could not wear his signature number 3 jersey on the Pistons, because the number was taken by guard Rodney Stuckey—who actually wore the number in Iverson's honor—and the league prohibited in-season changes. Stubborn, unwilling to accept a lesser role on the team, and hampered by back problems that caused him to miss sixteen consecutive games, he was clashing with rookie head coach Michael Curry. Curry alienated his two shooting guards, Iverson and Rip Hamilton, by bringing first Hamilton, and then Iverson off the bench. After four games as a reserve and numerous complaints about his role on the team, Iverson was declared out for the season with a bad back.

After a summer of looking for various opportunities at resurrecting his NBA career or just redeeming the failed episode on the Pistons, Iverson signed with the Grizzlies for $3.1 million, which was a substantial decrease in salary from the $21 million he made in Detroit the previous season. The Grizzlies were reportedly aiming to trade for the player in 2006, when he was shopped around by the Sixers. Lack of team success and the player's unwillingness to practice, combined with his late-night partying, were grounds for frustration on both sides. Sixers general manager Billy King was looking for a landing spot for Iverson and Memphis would have been perfect if not for the fact that, at the time, Michael Heisley was looking for a buyer for the Grizzlies. Team president Jerry West was not allowed to even entertain the possibility of trading for the equal-parts talented and troublesome guard,[22] with the franchise on the market—his contract would severely impact the team's cap space, hence the prospective owners' financial flexibility. Three years later, with a new team executive in place, the Grizzlies got Iverson for a far better price, but he was no longer the same player. Iverson was traded to the Nuggets, and for two seasons led the league in minutes and was among league leaders in points—which was no small feat when sharing the court with equally ball-dominant and trigger-happy Carmelo Anthony—but then he was traded to the Pistons, and his stay in Michigan exposed the flaws in his game.

High-profile teams were reluctant to guarantee him big minutes, knowing that he had lost a few steps, yet was not willing to adapt his game accordingly. Instead, he continued to post on social media how back in shape and NBA-ready he was, but he only got one offer—from the Memphis Grizzlies. Because of that, it is hard to evaluate the role location played in his decision-making process. In a way, however, joining the team gave him a chance to go full circle, as he grew up in neighboring Virginia, a half-day's drive from Memphis, in Hampton. During his introductory press conference, a fan reminded Iverson of his roots, when he called him by his childhood nickname "Bubba Chuck," and then told a story about his deceased son being a fan. The question/confession was described as a "weird, awkward moment" by *The Commercial Appeal*'s Chris Herrington, who added that it was the last time the Grizzlies allowed fans to ask questions during a presser.[23]

During his first press conference as a Grizzly, visibly touched, Iverson said: "This year for me is personal, it's basically going to be my rookie season again."[24] *The Commercial Appeal*'s Scott Cacciola wrote that the two sides wanted something from each other, "the Grizzlies, the faltering franchise, wanted a veteran star. Iverson, the fading icon, wanted another shot."[25] The Grizzlies had missed out on the postseason three seasons in a row and were dead last in attendance twice during that period. They were undeterred by the disappointing attendance and still did their part for the local community. In their inaugural season in Memphis, they gave away over fourteen thousand tickets to children via their Tickets for Kids program. In their second season in Memphis, they became partners with St. Jude Children's Research Hospital by donating $5 million to build the Memphis Grizzlies House to provide one hundred families with rooms for short and longer stays. In 2008, shooting guard Mike Miller and his family donated $200,000 to the hospital and to honor that contribution, the hospital named its exercise room after the Miller's two sons.

Iverson, a surefire Hall of Fame inductee, missed the first three games of the season for his new team, as he was recovering from a hamstring injury. With Grizzlies in the middle of a West Coast road trip, he appeared in the next three games, against the Kings, the Warriors, and the Lakers. In all three, he came off the bench, and then was granted permission to leave the team by owner Michael Heisley because of a personal issue. Just like Iverson, Heisley attended Georgetown—and in 1960, unlike Iverson, graduated from the university—so there was a mutual connection between the two. That the team owner informed the press about granting the player permission to leave signified that he was the one interested in signing Iverson and keeping him happy. Prior to the move, Heisley was talking about a three-year plan of getting the Grizzlies back to the playoffs, but once the player became available, he was willing to sign him, oblivious to other teams' lack of interest in the guard. Heisley wanted to discuss playing time with Iverson and made sure that the player knew he would be coming off the bench; but he backed out of the idea, scared that Iverson would not sign with the team.[26]

The official reasons for his absence with the Grizzlies were doubted; already after his first game, asked about whether his hamstring was still a problem, he answered: "I had a problem with my butt sitting on the bench so long. That's the only thing I had a problem with."[27] He also talked about starting at either guard position, with the Grizzlies' young starters he was supposed to mentor, Michael Conley and O. J. Mayo, sitting next to him. After the game against the Lakers, he asked the media to stop focusing on his complaints and write more about his teammates. Then, just like that, he was gone. He left for Atlanta, where his family was living, to take care of his sick daughter. After ten days away from the team, he was released. Less than ten days later, he announced his retirement, adding that he still wanted to play professional basketball.

Nine days later, Iverson's professional career really went full circle, as he signed with the Sixers for a nonguaranteed minimum contract after guard Lou Williams went down with a serious injury. The Sixers were bad, and Iverson calibrated by having the worst season of his career. He was voted into the All-Star Team as a starter, making the team for the eleventh season in a row. He missed it due to personal reasons and on March 2, 2010, it was announced, after a longer absence from the team, that he would no longer be part of the Sixers. His failure on the Grizzlies was just seen as a consequence of his personality, as the same things that made him great, the relentless attitude and unwillingness to conform, also led to his disappointing tenure in Memphis.

Francis and Iverson represent two very different examples of Grizzlies' history. There is no doubt who was the superior player, just as there is no doubt who had a larger impact on the franchise. Francis's snub largely contributed to professional basketball's failure in Vancouver, while the flop of one of the most popular athletes of the twenty-first century in Memphis did not tarnish the franchise's reputation. In fact, after a 1–8 start, the Grizzlies finished the season with forty wins. Both players went full circle in their professional careers, and while both would probably like a retake on the endings, it was as close to storybook as life gets.

As a rookie, Francis unknowingly contributed to his future teammate and mentor, Hakeem Olajuwon, not fulfilling his dream of retiring in Vancouver. The Nigerian-born center was a Houston basketball legend, a two-time NBA champion and 1994 league MVP. He also had family members and friends in Vancouver, whom he visited often. When asked in 1995, after winning back-to-back championships, whether he would retire in Houston, Olajuwon said: "I'm still not sure, because I like Vancouver also. That might not be a bad place to do it, because I loved this city before it even had a team."[28] In the summer of 2001, with the

Allen Iverson appeared in just three games for the Grizzlies.

Rockets in no position to contend for the playoffs, let alone a championship, he asked for a trade and was shipped to the Raptors, who since that season were the sole Canadian franchise in the NBA. He probably would not have joined the Grizzlies anyway, as the team was in an even worse predicament than the Rockets. In Toronto, Olajuwon played for Lenny Wilkens, whom the Grizzlies' executives rejected as potential head coach. If things had turned out differently, the two Hall of Famers would have become Vancouver sports royalty.

Upon signing Iverson, team owner Michael Heisley said: "I hope Memphis likes him. I really hope they respond to him. I think he's going to be outstanding."[29] While the Grizzlies' poor play was partially the result of their struggle for fan appreciation following the disassembling of the playoff-contending roster, their owner was not without blame. In 2006, just five years after moving the team, the *Forbes* 400–listed billionaire was looking to trade the team, which was reporting $40 million losses. With losses of such magnitude, the franchise's tumultuous history was in danger of repeating itself.

Chapter 5

The Most Hated Man in the City

The fans in Memphis would have probably much rather have had the Hornets than the Grizzlies. Both franchises announced that they wanted to relocate to Tennessee, but the Charlotte Hornets had a much better team and a richer history. They once had a promising core of power forward Larry Johnson and center Alonzo Mourning, but the team owner's unwillingness to pay the latter what he wanted made the center move to Miami. In the search for a starting big man, in the 1997 NBA Draft, the Hornets picked Kobe Bryant for the Lakers, with the thirteenth pick, and in exchange got Laker Vlade Divac, who considered retirement after being traded to North Carolina. His agent said: "If he's traded Monday, he will announce his retirement Tuesday."[1] Divac eventually left the team in free agency after two seasons. He was one of twenty-two consecutive free agents who rejected the Hornets contract proposals.[2]

Hornets owner George Shinn was infamous for his unwillingness to pay his employees. Dave Cowens, who coached the Hornets in the years 1996–99 and took the team to the playoffs twice, was the lowest-paid head coach in the league. The team offered him an extension, only to back out of it, because according to Shinn he "wasn't appreciative enough"[3] of the offer. The coach left, and in 2001 Hornets were in the midst of another successful rebuilt, with promising point guard Baron Davis and center Jamaal Magloire, as well as veterans David Wesley, P. J. Brown, Jamal Mashburn, and Elden Campbell on the roster. They were just one win away from the Eastern Conference Finals, losing to the Bucks in seven games.

However, they had an owner who alienated the fanbase. Shinn was accused of kidnapping and assaulting one woman, while another, a Hornets

cheerleader, claimed that he coerced her into a two-year-long sexual relationship, as she was afraid of losing her job if she refused his advances.
The 1999 trial between her and her former employer was broadcast on
national television and brought unwanted attention to the team. Despite
the on-court success of the Hornets, attendance dropped from around
24,000 in the first eight seasons, to 15,010 fans per game in 2000–01.
Shinn demanded a new arena from the city, even though he was not
paying taxes or living in Charlotte. The local business and city leaders
were willing to consider building the new arena if he would contribute
$13 million of his own money. He declined on the account that he did not
have that much. He decided to move the franchise.

Apart from Memphis, Norfolk, Louisville, and New Orleans were
strongly considered as potential relocation spots. Memphis and New
Orleans were the only locations with arenas that the team could immediately inhabit, which put them at the forefront of the bidding
war. Furthermore, Hornets co-owner Ray Wooldridge was a native of
Memphis. In July 1999, he bought a 35 percent stake in the Hornets.
In 2004, Shinn would buy back his share and regain complete control
over the team. The Hornets eventually moved to New Orleans in 2002.
The New Orleans Arena came with $10 million for immediate upgrades
and a couple of million annually thanks to the local arena hotel tax. The
most important thing for Shinn, whose Hornets were reportedly losing around $1 million a month in Charlotte, was that as opposed to the
Charlotte Coliseum which had twelve business suites, the New Orleans
Arena had forty-four and room for twenty more.[4]

The Grizzlies had relocated to Memphis a year earlier, in 2001, and
while there was at a certain point a proposal for the teams swapping
owners, so that Shinn and Wooldridge would take over the Tennessee
transplant, while Michael Heisley, who bought the Grizzlies in 2000,
would do his best to keep the franchise in Charlotte, nothing came of
it. The Grizzlies kicked off their first home game in Memphis with pop-
star Justin Timberlake performing the national anthem and Isaac Hayes
singing "God Bless America." The two performers represented the dual-
istic nature of the city, as the white Timberlake stood for its clean-cut,
"mainstream" potential while Black Hayes was "a symbol of Black mil-
itancy" in the 1970s, and remained one of the most recognizable funk

and soul singers in America.[5] Head coach Sidney Lowe said of the city: "I think of Memphis, I think of basketball. That's the kind of city this is."[6] While it made sense to view Memphis as a basketball town, and the celebrities appearing at the event were supposed to solidify that notion, this perception applied to college basketball, as professional ball had until that point little success in the city.

Keith B. Wood in *Memphis Hoops. Race and Basketball in the Bluff City, 1968–1997*, notes that basketball played a big part in the narratives of integration, as they presented the city as connected with the aid of the sport. This myth originated in 1969, during the MIAA City Championship, where the all-white Overton faced the all-Black Melrose High and truly blossomed during Memphis State's run to the 1973 NCAA final game, where the team fell to Bill Walton's mighty UCLA. Melrose High and Memphis State teams were led by two African American players, Larry Finch and Ronnie Robinson, while the face of Overton was white Johnny Neumann. Wood notes that "basketball gave the people a temporary common ground where the hopes of white and Black people were played out in front of them."[7]

That myth was disrupted by the failure of professional basketball in the city. For years, the sport seemed to avoid Memphis—except for a couple of exhibition games here and there. For example, the barnstorming professional team the New York Celtics had visited the state annually since 1926, first coming to Nashville, and three years later to Memphis, showcasing their "wonderful passing system" and shooting "from all sections of the floor with amazing accuracy."[8] The Celtics were unbeaten in Memphis, and would even beat the Akron Firestones, the reigning National Basketball League champions in the Ellis Auditorium to amass a 13–0 record in the Bluff City. The venue was capable of housing around 10,000 fans, while around 4,300 people watched the contest.[9] Opened in 1930, the auditorium was named after Robert R. Ellis, who advocated for the construction of the municipal building, which would bring thousands of people to Memphis for various events.

The major leagues however had steadily ignored Memphis as a long-term destination. As Wood pointed out: "The instability of Memphis's ABA franchise mirrors the political instability that was present in the city during this same period. The failure of the ABA to prosper in the city in the 1970s speaks to an underlying racial discord. The ABA franchise's five-year stay in town provides a counter-narrative to the myth that basketball was able to heal the city's racial woes."[10] The American Basketball Association originated as a football league, but its founder, Dennis Murphy, concluded that it would be easier to challenge the NBA, which was one professional league, as opposed to the NFL and the AFL, which the upstart football league would have to face.[11] The 1967 NBA had twelve teams, and the ABA started its inaugural season, 1967–68, with eleven teams. One of the cities awarded a franchise was New Orleans, where the Buccaneers were able to dominate thanks to the offensive duo of Larry Brown and Doug Moe, who would both become great NBA coaches. When reminiscing about the early years of the league, Brown said: "Guys were told to brown-bag it so they would have something to eat. . . . We had 12 players at home, but only traveled 10 to save on the airline, meal and hotel bills. Really, it was a struggle."[12] Despite the unfavorable conditions, the Buccaneers won at least 50 percent of their games in the three seasons they spent in New Orleans.

In 1970, real estate magnate P. L. Blake bought the franchise and moved it to Memphis. In a move intended to set the identity of the relocated franchise, but also to cut costs, he renamed the team "Pros" and replaced the abbreviated "Bucs" nickname on their old jerseys with their new name, instead of simply providing the franchise with new gear.[13] The Pros played only thirty-one games in Memphis, because the schedule was announced prior to the relocation, and the arena was booked for the other eleven games. The move was ill-fated from the start, with the team being unable to note a winning season in its four years in Memphis or build a loyal fanbase that would actually attend home games.

The Pros/Tams/Sounds—the franchise changed its name three times —played at Mid-South Coliseum, erected in the 1960s in midtown Memphis to serve as the entertainment and sports venue across seven states (Arkansas, Alabama, Kentucky, Mississippi, Missouri, Oklahoma, and Tennessee). The construction, which began in 1963, was one of a series of investments intended to revitalize the city. The Memphis Municipal Airport was renamed Memphis Metropolitan Airport following the construction of a new terminal in 1963. Skyscrapers, including the First Tennessee Building and 100 North Main, were erected around the same time. A new municipal center was also being developed. More importantly, from a sports perspective, a fifty-thousand-seat stadium was constructed next to the arena.

The first tenants of the Mid-South Coliseum were the Memphis Wings of the Central Hockey League, the farm team of the Detroit Red Wings of the National Hockey League. The Pros were the second Coliseum-based franchise. Less than two months into the team's first regular season in Memphis, the owner reported $200,000 losses and put it up for sale. It was bought by community group Memphis Area Sports Inc. for $700,000, just as it was about to fold. In a last-chance effort, the Pros installed a twenty-four-hour answering service for pledges. The team still had a chance of making the playoffs when the talks with the prospective owners started, but the ownership change was completed after the Pros were eliminated from playoff contention by the Pacers in four games.

It was important to keep the team in the city, because civic boosters believed that if a professional basketball team failed after one season, a professional football team would never come to Memphis.[14] A football franchise was the next logical move if a city wanted to become big time. Furthermore, there was pressure on the Pros to stay in Memphis, due to the inevitable NBA-ABA merger, which had been talked about for a number of years. Woodrow Paige Jr. of *The Commercial Appeal* wrote about the excitement in the city for the arrival of the NBA, predicting that the new league would consist of twenty-eight teams.[15] Herb Kosten, president of Memphis Area Sports Inc., said that the merger "will make it easier for the Memphis Pros to make it in Memphis, and that has been our primary goal since the start."[16]

In the next season, the Pros dropped from forty-one wins to twenty-six. A year later, they won only twenty-one games and were once again a step away from folding. This is when Charles O. Finley entered the scene. He already owned the NHL's California Golden Seals and AL's Oakland Athletics, whom he moved from Kansas City just two years earlier, in 1968. Finley talked a big game, but also went out of his way to deliver on his promises. Wood writes that "fans were hopeful that Finley's determination to win, his desire to outwork his opponents, and his creative marketing ploys would be enough to steady the franchise."[17] On September 17, 1964, he gave the Beatles $150,000 for a charity concert in Kansas City during their first American tour. Kansas City was not one of the planned stops on the tour, and Finley needed to dig deep into his pockets to convince the band to play a couple of their songs in Kansas. The A's were still in Kansas City at the time.

Now he was looking for an ABA team, regardless of the location. One of the first orders of business was changing the name of the franchise. Out of a couple of proposals, Finley picked the Memphis Tams, which stood for Tennessee, Arkansas, and Mississippi (TAMs), because the owner hoped for the team to draw interest from the fans from these three states, while also referencing Tam O'Shanter, the hero of a poem by Robert Burns. The name of the franchise was therefore supposed to honor the city's Scottish heritage.[18]

The team continued to play badly and the local fans were not particularly enthusiastic about coming to games and rooting for a losing franchise. After two seasons, with Finley regularly complaining about the team, and expressing his willingness to trade it away, as well as give it away, it was taken over by the league. In 1974, ABA commissioner Mike Storen resigned from his function and became the owner of the team. He justified his decision years later to Terry Pluto as follows: "The league decided that two years of Finley was more than enough. The league had been more or less running the franchise anyway, because Charlie had stopped paying the bills."[19]

A week after Storen took over the team, he renamed it the Memphis Sounds, which he considered a more appropriate name for a team from a city with such a rich musical history. Music, just as sport, was seen as a unifying force in a historically segregated town, with artists such as Elvis Presley or Isaac Hayes overcoming racial barriers. Hayes was also a member of the investment group that took over the team. The Sounds were in financial trouble from the beginning, and during the 1974–75 season, the three biggest potential investors backed out—apart from Hayes, there were Avron Fogelman and Kemmonis Wilson. After just one season, the franchise relocated to Baltimore, where it died out without playing a single ABA game. Before that happened, the Sounds somewhat surprisingly made the 1975 playoffs, despite winning just twenty-seven games during the regular season. They fell in five games to the eventual ABA Champions, the Kentucky Colonels. A year later, the ABA-NBA merger happened. The franchise waited five years for its sole playoff win, and the lack of playoff success would carry over to the relocated Grizzlies as well, who had to wait ten seasons for their first postseason win.

The history of professional basketball in Memphis was not a proud one, but the fact that it even existed allowed the NBA to prove that the relocation to Tennessee was not accidental. On December 9, 2005, the Grizzlies wore the throwback Pros uniforms to the home game against the Mavericks, where the crowd of 17,176 watched the team lose 90–83. When in February of 2012, nine NBA teams celebrated the founding of the ABA by sporting the outfits of franchises from the same region, Memphis was among them. During the NBA Hardwood Classics Month, the Grizzlies wore the yellow and green Memphis Tams uniforms. In the 2015–16 season, the Grizzlies debuted the throwback Memphis Sounds uniforms, paying homage to the franchise that failed in the city. On five game nights, the fans were invited to "step back into the era of funk, afros, bell-bottoms and enjoy the fresh vibe of music, giveaways and promotions," per the team's official website.

While the Grizzlies were a transplant, the name itself already had a place in the city's sports history. The World Football League's Memphis Southmen were nicknamed the Grizzlies, because their logo featured a brown grizzly against an orange, sun-shaped background. The franchise was able to set the record for most tickets sold in a day for any event held at the city's fifty-thousand-seat Memphis Memorial Stadium with over ten thousand. The Southmen were a transplant from Canada as well, as they were originally the Northmen, based in Toronto. Memphis took in the team after an eight-year courtship of the NFL failed in 1974, with Tampa Bay and Seattle emerging as the only next league-expansion locations. A week later, the Northmen moved south. They folded in 1975 during an incomplete regular season, along with the whole WFL, due to the league's financial difficulties. It turned out that multiple WFL teams had lied about the number of tickets they sold.

Michael Heisley, who bought the Grizzlies for $160 million in January of 2000 (while the takeover was approved on April 11, 2000) from John McCaw, promised that the team would stay in Vancouver. He knew how league commissioner David Stern felt about franchises moving: "I know that David Stern does not like to see franchises relocate, I think every-one associated with the NBA sees it as a failure."[20] In February of 2001, Heisley filed the paperwork necessary for relocation. When he bought the team, it was reporting losses of $20 million per season, after 2000–01 they were up to $40 million. Player and staff salaries were paid in US dollars, ticket revenue was in Canadian dollars, and the exchange rate was around 1.4–1.5 for the first five years of the Grizzlies' existence. This calculation was especially hurtful for a franchise that failed to garner any interest outside the local market.

Before officially acquiring the Grizzlies, Heisley said he would be will-ing to exceed the league salary cap of $34 million if it could bring a cham-pionship to Vancouver,[21] but the rapidly shrinking fanbase convinced him otherwise. The average attendance of 12,626 per game would drop to 4,800 during the last games of the 1999–2000 season. Colin Jones of the University of Victoria claimed that the reason behind the failure of professional basketball in Vancouver was the quality of the team: "The way to attract people to any sport, you have either a winning or a com-petitive team. They don't have a very good team."[22] This was an under-statement. The Grizzlies had a terrible team, and its lone star, Shareef Abdur-Rahim, had just filed a trade request, stating that he would not stay on the Grizzlies if general manager Stu Jackson was to be fired by the new owner. This position earned him the ire of the league estab-lishment, including Phil Jackson, at the time coaching league champi-ons, the Lakers: "In our business, players can't run this business. People that do this have to be able to run the business because there's just too many decisions to be made."[23] Abdur-Rahim felt indebted to Stu Jackson for the six-year, $71 million deal he signed the forward to in January of 1999. For his part, Jackson was grateful to the player for saving his job, as Abdur-Rahim was one of only two reliable players—the other being Mike Bibby—picked by Jackson in the NBA Draft. The player's agent, Aaron Goodwin, understood that the decision to prolong the deal came at a price: "Right now Shareef is one of the most recognizable athletes in Canada, but athletes aren't marketed in Canada as they are in the U.S. We need not just our partnerships with Nike, but we need Grizzlies and their corporate sponsorships to help get Grizzlies' basketball out there."[24] None of that happened, and the team continued to struggle for attention outside of basketball circles.

When attention came, it was only for negative reasons. Heisley's declarations about paying out of his own pocket for the Grizzlies to be competitive were immediately treated with skepticism, as he refused to increase the $250,000 salary of assistant coach Lionel Hollins after he was promoted to the interim position. Jackson wanted to pay Hollins $700,000, which would still make him one of the lowest-paid coaches in the NBA. Former NCAA and NBA coach Dick Versace served as Heisley's basketball advisor, and it was rumored that he would take over either Jackson's or Hollins's job. He was the brother of Heisley's best friend, H. R. Versace, who died in Vietnam.

Heisley was simply waiting for league approval to make any roster and staff moves, but his overtly patient approach stood in contrast to the style of billionaire Mark Cuban, who bought the Dallas Mavericks in December of 1999 and was also waiting for league approval. Unlike Heisley, Cuban attended every game of his not-yet team and influenced roster moves. In fact, he was mingling with his players pre-games and sitting behind the bench during contests. The Grizzlies' veteran guard Doug West said: "That's something that needs to be done for the franchise to be successful."[25] Heisley was not doing any of that.

Hollins eventually received an additional $400,000 for his work as head coach, even though it was certain that he would be gone once the season was over. He took over the team from Brian Hill after a 4–18 start, and coached it to a franchise-record twenty-two wins. "Coached" may have been too big of a word at times, as during the contract dispute, in the game against the Rockets on April 4, 2000, Hollins allowed his players to call their own plays and barely got out of his seat. The Grizzlies won 102–100, despite trailing by as many as 18 points in the third quarter.[26] At the end of the season Hollins was indeed fired, by phone, and Jackson resigned a day after Hollins was shown the door. Versace became the president of basketball operations, Billy Knight was named the new general manager, and Tony Barone, the director of player personnel. Barone was, just like Heisley, a native of Chicago. Billy Knight was a former NBA player who previously worked for the Indiana Pacers.

In large part due to Vince Carter's spectacular and efficient play, the Raptors gained global popularity and the franchise was able to remain and become successful in Toronto.

Legendary NBA coach Chuck Daly, who guided the Detroit Pistons to two championships and the original Dream Team to Olympic gold in 1992, was brought in as an advisor, working remotely from his Florida home. None of the men had any local ties.

Granted, the "neighboring" Toronto Raptors also lacked any players or executives with Canadian ties, they were locally owned by Maple Leaf Sports and Entertainment, and the company cared about keeping the Raptors in Toronto. The Vancouver-based Orca Bay Sports and Entertainment was run by Seattle-based businessman John McCaw Jr., who bought the company from Arthur Griffiths on November 12, 1996. Originally he was Griffith's partner, holding 30 percent of the company, while the Vancouver businessman controlled the rest. Due to company reporting losses, Griffiths put up the Grizzlies, the Canucks, and the GM Place for sale. The Grizzlies' losses were relatively modest in comparison to the Canucks, who lost about $100 million in four years. McCaw made it known that he expected the new owner to keep both franchises in Vancouver.[27] He even reportedly had a handshake deal with Missoula businessman Dennis Washington, who would purchase 50 percent of Orca Bay and keep the two franchises in Vancouver.[28]

Soon, McCaw almost sold the franchise in late 1999 to Bill Laurie, who had recently bought the NHL's St. Louis Blues and the Kiel Center, where the Blues played. Prior to bidding for the Grizzlies, he attempted to buy the Denver Nuggets earlier in the year (for $400 million), and considered buying the Charlotte Hornets a year later. While Laurie never explicitly said that he wanted to move the team to St. Louis, it was more or less clear why he attempted the purchase. Bernie Miklasz of the *St. Louis Post-Dispatch* characterized Laurie as "the Donald Trump of sports. He wants it, he buys it."[29] This time though Laurie would not have his way.

Upon learning of the proposed move, former Vancouver mayor Art Phillips organized a "We Love Our Grizzlies" campaign, intended to keep the Grizzlies in the city. David Stern and the NBA also urged Laurie to restructure the deal in order to do everything possible to keep the Grizzlies in Vancouver. Prominent team owners, like Jerry Buss of the Los Angeles Lakers and Jerry Colangelo of the Phoenix Suns, also spoke in support of the team remaining in Canada. On January 20, 2000, four months after he announced the acquisition, Laurie backed out of the deal via a press release, in which he admitted that he bought the Grizzlies with the intention of relocating to St. Louis, and McCaw knew it from the start. The still-owner claimed he sold the franchise under the condition it would stay in Vancouver.

Just four days later, out of nowhere, Heisley was announced as the new owner. Art Phillips said the fans in Vancouver were indebted to David Stern and McCaw for their willingness to continue searching for a prospective owner willing to keep the Grizzlies in Canada. Phillips was also tasked with marketing the team to the fans. Less than a year later, he described Heisley's taking over the franchise as a "bloody plot" and called the new owner "a snake."[30]

Heisley announced his acquisition at a press conference, during which he introduced himself as "Mike Heisley from Chicago" and soon put on a Grizzlies jacket, which he referred to as "the most expensive leather coat in Canada."[31] Heisley loved hard work and presented himself as part of the working class. He grew up in Alexandria, Virginia, where his parents worked on the railroad. A self-made man, in the 1970s, he sold his house and bought a company selling sewer-cleaning equipment. He proudly spoke about being a fan of the Chicago Bulls before Michael Jordan came to the city and turned them into a winner. Heisley was known as a man of the people, buying struggling companies and taking care of the workers who were already there.[32] He was expected to do the same in Vancouver.

After the 1999–2000 season, Versace took over personnel duties and named Sidney Lowe, the Timberwolves' assistant, as head coach. Lowe's job interview was ten hours long, and he blew away Versace and Knight with his basketball knowledge. It was his second chance to be the head coach of a professional basketball team, following less than two seasons on the Timberwolves' bench in the years 1992–94.

The summer of 2000 would turn out to be crucial for keeping the Grizzlies in Vancouver. With the second overall pick, they selected Stromile Swift, an athletic dunker whose on-court exploits could (hopefully) rival those of Vince Carter. The Raptors employed a new head coach during the same time as the Grizzlies. They picked Lenny Wilkens, at the time the winningest coach in league history—in twenty-seven seasons his teams won 1,179 games. He was known for turning around small- and mid-market franchises—the Sonics, the Blazers, the Cavs, and the Hawks. An experienced, well-leveled coach would serve the Grizzlies well, and indeed Wilkens wanted to work in Vancouver; but Versace preferred Lowe, so Wilkens joined the Raptors. In his first season in Toronto, the team was one win away from Eastern Conference Finals. Versace would suggest during that same season that the Grizzlies would have won more games with an experienced coach, even though he was the one who had picked Lowe over Wilkens.

The problem with Swift was that, although the twenty-one-year-old out of LSU could be spectacular, his play did not justify that high of a selection. It was only after the Grizzlies traded starting power forward Othella Harrington to the Knicks that Swift's minutes increased, as he found himself fighting for playing time with veteran Grant Long. Mike Bibby and Shareef Abdur-Rahim continued to play steadily, as did twenty-five-year-old shooting guard Michael Dickerson. The three players led the team in minutes per game. The same could not be said of the front-court players, with Reeves coming off the bench in twenty-seven games, behind either Isaac Austin or journeyman Tony Massenburg, and the power forward spot being handled by Harrington, Long, and Swift. Heisley seriously considered bringing in thirty-nine-year-old Dennis Rodman to garner publicity, but his failed stint on the Mavericks during the previous season—he averaged 14.3 rebounds per game, but was a distraction and a bad influence on the team's younger players and was cut after twelve games—eventually discouraged the owner from bringing in the five-time NBA Champion.

During the 2000–01 season opener, the new owner performed the Canadian national anthem, with fans cheering in the stands. Three months later, in January, Heisley complained to the press about how hard it was for him to keep the Grizzlies in Vancouver, and openly discussed selling the team. He also spoke about how embarrassing it would have been for him to move the team, and how much pressure he felt for the franchise to remain in Canada.[33] In February of 2001, when asked about the team playing in Vancouver in the next season, he replied: "I cannot honestly answer that question."[34] He met with the league commissioner during the All-Star Game. After the meeting, Stern, who was so adamant about the team moving from Vancouver, approved the decision

Mike Bibby, an NCAA Champion with the Arizona Wildcats, endured a lot of losing when playing for the Grizzlies.

to relocate. The ease with which Stern gave up on basketball in British Columbia, after defending it so vehemently in the past, was somewhat surprising.

Heisley singled out four potential destinations for relocation: Louisville, Anaheim, New Orleans, and Memphis. At one point, he even considered the suburbs of his hometown Chicago, but the locals were not interested. The offer from Louisville would include a $200 million arena that would be sponsored by Kentucky Fried Chicken. The company also proposed that the new arena be named the KFC Bucket and the team go by the Kentucky Colonels,[35] in a callback to the ABA's Kentucky Colonels and a way of honoring KFC's founder, Colonel Harlan Sanders. Stern was not necessarily willing for the team to move to Anaheim, as California already had four NBA teams, the most out of all the states. The last NBA team to relocate were the Sacramento Kings, who in fact moved to California from Kansas City in 1985. The two teams willing to relocate, the Grizzlies and the Hornets, set their sights on Memphis. While Heisley was very public about relocation and talks with American cities, Shinn and Wooldridge submitted their bid somewhat surprisingly.

Meanwhile, Heisley became "the most hated man in the city"—at least that was how he described himself—for wanting to move the franchise, while continuing to complain to the press that he was waiting for an offer from a group from Vancouver to buy the team, and expressing the desire to sit courtside during one of the remaining four home games.[36] A total of 18,571 fans attended the Grizzlies' last home game, against the Houston Rockets. Fittingly, they faced off against the player who snubbed them on 1999 draft night, Steve Francis. Against the Grizzlies, he played almost 41 minutes, scored 14 points, and dished out 13 assists. He also made four of 13 shots and had six turnovers.

As usual, he would earn jeers from the local fans, who were visibly frustrated that this was the last game in Vancouver. However, Francis was not the focal point of their anger, at least not this time. "Heisley sucks" was the chorus that carried on throughout the whole game. Most sports fans in the city were watching the Canucks play the Colorado Avalanche in the first playoff series in Vancouver in five years. Some showed up to the game to vent their frustration. A couple of months later, Heisley expressed regret about how he handled the relocation, adding, "Had I been a fan in Vancouver, I would have been out there with them, booing Michael Heisley."[37]

Some players took off their jerseys and gave them away. Shareef Abdur-Rahim, the best player in the franchise's brief history, who also at one point demanded a trade, addressed the home fans. The same fans got their season tickets in paper envelopes, after buying them without any marketing campaign preceding the season in which Vancouver was to fight for its franchise; $5,000 worth of tickets came without any thank you notes, yet the franchise sold almost five thousand such parcels.[38] The team was never good, even decent. The closest it came to providing the City of Vancouver with a sense of pride was during their last season there, when they won five games in a row. Unfortunately, they had twice lost nineteen games in a row (during their first and last seasons in Vancouver), as well as twelve or more games in a row four more times. Their last season in Vancouver was also their best; but with twenty-three wins it did not seem that big of an achievement. During their last season, they had also won their hundredth game in franchise history. It took them six years to reach that milestone, and they won one game more just for good measure, finishing their stay in Canada with 101 wins and 359 losses.

And yet they were supported by more than thirteen thousand fans per game. When in February of 2001 David Stern said that "it's unfortunate that the city with that kind of resources had not rallied behind the club,"[39] he was being selfish and unfair, because the franchise did very little to endear itself to the community. Just consider the above-mentioned disappointing season ticket parcels sent out during the most important year in the franchise's existence. It is always said that loyal fans support their teams through thick and thin. Year after year, the Grizzlies' fans learned a lesson on having an NBA franchise—winning alone may not save a franchise, but it sure is helpful in keeping it alive.

Chapter 6

Bears in the Pyramid

In a December 2006 interview with *The Commercial Appeal*, the Grizzlies owner, Michael Heisley, expressed his intention to part with one of his prized possessions, stating: "Somebody can do a better job than I can with the franchise. I'm being very honest with myself. Unlike a lot of NBA owners, I'm not putting in 100 percent of my time. I'm almost 70 years of age so I'm not likely to get more of it."[1] While it was hard to doubt the sincerity of Heisley's intentions, the owner was once again willing to dispose of the franchise when it was struggling, just as he had in Vancouver. Since the league would not allow the Grizzlies to simply fold—and according to the deal signed with the city they could not relocate for ten years, Heisley was stuck with the franchise if no potential buyer appeared. Rather, he was stuck with his 70 percent, as 30 percent belonged to the Memphis community, which invited the team to the city and welcomed it with great enthusiasm. The $250 million that the taxpayers shelled out for the new arena did not hurt either.

FedEx Corp., a Memphis-based global shipping company, not so much offered as promised that it would buy team- and arena-naming rights when the Grizzlies moved from Vancouver. The company's executive vice president and chief financial officer, Alan B. Graf Jr., spoke about the company's aggressive pursuit of getting a professional basketball franchise to Memphis, adding as an upside that the company had forty-thousand local employees and "a tremendous amount of knowledge about how not to just put a name on an arena and a team, but how to market it."[2] FedEx already had a sponsorship deal with the USA Basketball team, and naming rights to the former Washington Redskins' playing field. The proposal that the company e-mailed to Heisley was

twenty pages long, single spaced.[3] While Memphis was the strongest
candidate for the relocation spot, due to the seriousness of the offer and
the big-company financial backing, the Grizzlies' owner, not wanting
to alienate other cities, refused responsibility for the selection, saying:
"[David Stern] is going to make all the announcements. . . . He's basically
controlling the thing now."[4]

The Memphis pursuit team, named Memphis Tomorrow, was led by
J. R. Hyde III, the grandson of Joseph Reeves Hyde Sr., who moved to
Memphis from Chattanooga in search of work, and a couple of years
later, in 1907, established Malone & Hyde, a food distribution company that eventually became one of America's biggest food wholesalers.
J. R. Hyde III, known simply as Pitt Hyde, was largely responsible for the
company's success. He took over the company as a twenty-six-year-old,
bought out some of its competition, and created an auto parts company
called AutoZone in 1979, as part of Malone & Hyde. In 1988, he separated
both companies, sold Malone & Hyde, and kept AutoZone. He retired
from the company in 1997 and completely devoted his efforts to local
philanthropy through Hyde Family Foundations. Along with his wife,
they were among the six investors intending to bring an NBA franchise
to the city. His wife, Barbara R. Hyde considered the process a prime
example of venture philanthropy, meaning that while the relocation bid
was organized as a business investment, it was not done for profit but "to
make a difference in this city."[5]

There was valid optimism that the franchise could indeed bring the
people together, and it was estimated that the local ownership group's
stake in the team could reach up to 50 percent (eventually it would reach
30). African American Charles L. Ewing Sr. became the first minority
member of the investor group. Ewing owned Ewing Moving Service Inc.,
a company that he established by himself in 1980 with just one pickup
truck. The second African American member of the investment group
was Fred Jones Jr., CEO of Summitt Management Corporation, who was,
inter alia, the road manager for Memphis singer Isaac Hayes and tour
manager for the Isley Brothers, before establishing his own company.
The unusual spelling of the word "summit" was supposed to represent
the uniqueness of the events organized by the company.

Pitt Hyde was the face and the voice of the pursuit team, but the man behind the push was Staley Cates, whom Hyde described as "far more knowledgeable on the subject."[6] During a June 2000 meeting with David Stern, Cates described Memphis as a one-franchise city that would rally around its sole professional team like Portland or San Antonio did. Cates was the thirty-seven-year-old president of international investment company Southeastern Asset Management Inc. who preferred to do things quietly, without fanfare. And that was how the pursuit of NBA basketball began—there was no big press conference, just interviews in newspapers and meetings. Lots and lots of meetings. Staley Cates and his younger brother Andy, who was a real estate developer, completed the six-person investment group, aided by philanthropist Gayle Rose and attorney Marty Regan.

The pursuit team did not want to step on anybody's toes so it met on January 15, 2000, with the most important basketball man in the city, John Calipari. The coach of the University of Memphis NCAA team was rebuilding the program, which has not produced a Final Four team since 1985 and had been out of the NCAA tournament for four seasons in a row. He was also rebuilding his reputation, hurt by his short but eventful time in the NBA. Calipari took over the New Jersey Nets in 1996, and in two years turned them into a playoff team, making the postseason for the first time in four years. Next season, the Nets got off to a 3–17 start and Calipari was fired. He joined the staff of his mentor, Larry Brown, on the Sixers as an assistant coach. It was Brown who convinced Calipari to take over the Memphis Tigers.[7]

Before he joined the Nets, Calipari took University of Massachusetts to the 1996 Final Four, and hopes were that he could do the same in Tennessee. The Tigers got off to the worst start since the 1968–69 season, going 4–8 in the first twelve games, but Calipari was showing the same relentlessness that would become a signature of the Grit & Grind Grizzlies. He was willing to put in time and effort to make the program work. After the game against Southern Mississippi, he said to the reporters: "This is a great diet. Look at my loose collar. If you think I'm down here collecting a paycheck, you're outta your mind, because it's driving me crazy."[8] He eventually turned the program around and became a beloved sports figure—At least until he left for Kentucky in 2008, when it was revealed that his star recruit had been admitted to Memphis with a fraudulent SAT score. As a result, the team's 2007–08 season-record thirty-eight wins were vacated. That star recruit was future NBA MVP Derrick Rose. Calipari believed that the two teams, amateur and professional, could exist not only in the same city, but also in the same arena. At least for some time the 20,142–seat Pyramid would house the Grizzlies and the Tigers, until the FedExForum could be built.

The Great American Pyramid, as the sports center was called, was a vision dreamed up by designer Mark Hartz, architect Robert Hall, and businessman Vance Stewart. Stewart and Hall presented the city and county officials with the proposal of three pyramid-shaped buildings in 1975, but were rejected. It was Hartz's son, Brent, who reintroduced the design in 1986, this time as a single building. Three to four thousand fans per year were left without season tickets for the Tigers, and the NCAA team was in desperate need of a new arena. The First Tennessee Bank building was lit with pyramid-shaped lights in the days leading up to the beginning of construction work, on September 15, 1989, a Friday night. Up until that point, the building was known for its Christmas light displays.[9] The Pyramid was supposed to be a vital part of the city landscape, rivaling St. Louis's Gateway Arch as a significant local landmark. More than the outlandish look, it was the sports arena that was important, at least from a basketball fan's perspective. The University of Memphis needed a bigger arena, and if it had to be pyramid-shaped to get the funding, so be it.

The construction of the thirty-one-story arena in downtown Memphis would be funded by the City Council and county Board of Commissioners, but only up to the $39 million mark. Everything exceeding the budget was supposed to be privately funded. A nine-member Pyramid Building Commission was tasked with developing a financial plan. Mayor Willie Herenton and Shelby county mayor Bill Morris picked the members of the commission—this was after Memphis State University (MSU) intended to go through with its own arena, which was supposed to cost $32.9 million and be built on campus. With not enough money for the construction of two arenas in the local budget, support for the Pyramid, which was to serve as a sport arena, a concert, and convention venue, gained traction.

The fact that Memphis State University—which would change its name to the University of Memphis on July 1, 1994—was supposed to have twenty-five free dates at the venue, made the victory for downtown boosters all the more certain. MSU president Thomas Carpenter commented on the issue diplomatically: "There were a number of reasons why the location downtown and the pyramid were not our first choice, but once we decided to go with it, then all these other things are out of consideration."[10]

The Pyramid was supposed to serve as an homage to the original Memphis, the ancient capital of Lower Egypt, from which the city got its name. It was not the first homage to Egypt in the city's recent history—in 1897, during the Tennessee Centennial Exposition in Nashville, the city's contribution was a one hundred-foot-tall Pyramid of Cheops. Vance Stewart, one of the three fathers of the original idea of the pyramid, was happy with how it turned out, but he still had some suggestions on improving the overall experience, like the daily changing of the guard of people dressed as Egyptian soldiers.[11] Stewart also wanted the building to be gilded. Instead, it was glass and stainless steel. On sunny days, the glassy building would reflect sunrays and cause a nuisance to drivers.

"The modern answer to the medieval cathedral," as the Pyramid was called, eventually cost $65 million. The fact that it was even completed was a miracle, as the construction was either doomed or cursed from the start. On Friday, September 15, 1989, rain postponed the Big Dig, as events surrounding the beginning of the construction were collectively called. The name Big Dig was not an understatement, as a fifty-foot-long shovel was flown from a helicopter and dropped down, while the sky was decorated with a laser-light pyramid. The event cost $440,000. The man responsible for staging the event was Sidney Shlenker, brought in by Memphis financier John Tigrett, just four months after he won local financial backing for the arena. Tigrett was on the board of Federal Express Corp., the company that would later get involved in bringing the Grizzlies to Memphis and buy the naming rights for the new arena. Eventually, to no one's surprise, the NBA would not allow the Grizzlies to be renamed after a corporate sponsor.

The 7–4 vote in favor of public funding for the Pyramid was made possible by a promise from Tigrett's son, Isaac Burton Tigrett, that

Hard Rock Café would open one of its bars in the building. Isaac Burton Tigrett was co-owner of the company, although not for long, because he would soon sell his stake without getting the new owner of Hard Rock Café, Robert Earl, to agree to follow through with the franchise opening in the Pyramid. As a result, Tigrett needed to pay twice the franchise price, which amounted to $2 million, to avoid legal action and keep the project from collapsing. Tigrett's signature was supposed to guarantee the minimum of $10 million public investment in the pyramid.

Shlenker, who had prior experience as chief executive officer of the Houston Astrodome, minority owner of the Houston Rockets, and owner of the Denver Nuggets, seemed like the perfect man for such an over-the-top project. In an article about the failure of the Pyramid's financing, Louis Graham recounts Shlenker's various unconventional actions: "Shlenker had paid $125 to swap airline seats with a stranger in order to meet Astrodome creator Judge Roy Hofheinz and wound up Astrodome president. He had coaxed motorcycle daredevil Evel Knievel from his trailer just moments before a scheduled jump at the dome. He had made $35 million on a single television deal. He had bought the Nuggets over the phone."[12] On April 14, 1989, Richard Hackett, serving as Memphis mayor since 1982, and Bill Morris, Shelby County mayor since 1978, signed management control of the Pyramid over to Shlenker. He promised he would raise $55 million from corporate sponsors to provide entertainment facilities inside the Pyramid and at the nearby park, Mud Island. Opened on July 4, 1982, the park was an homage to the Mississippi River, with its most interesting attraction being a miniature model of the river, which was also a walkway. There were also an amphitheater, an interactive river museum, shops, restaurants, and benches. Shlenker's business plan consisted of a number of linked deals that depended on each other, which meant that if one fell through, others would soon follow.

Shlenker was not accustomed to failure in his business endeavors. His father, Irving M. Shlenker, started off as a warehouse manager in Monroe, Mississippi, and when he died in 1967, he left assets of $4.25 million, including stock in Malone & Hyde Inc.[13] His son worked in his father's bank in Houston, until he quit to establish and run, along with Allan Becker, Pace Management Corp. in 1965. The younger Shlenker found his calling in organizing events, like concerts, races, and variety shows. When running the Astrodome, he organized boxing fights as well as the "Battle of the Sexes," the 1973 tennis match between Billy Jean King and Bobby Riggs. He developed a reputation of a man who could stage events that would bring in substantial revenue.

Shlenker promised three million tourists a year to the city officials. Memphis lawyer Bill Haltom recounted Shlenker's numerous faults: he sold the rights to sell food and drinks to various companies, but did not build concession stands for them; he collected a year's rent in advance for private suites, but did not build the suites; he started a private club, collected membership fees, but did not bother to build the club.[14] Pizza Hut alone committed $30 million to the project in three separate deals. His proposed modifications of Mud Island were equally intriguing, as he wanted to connect the Pyramid to the park, forming what he called the Rakapolis experience, which "would ferry those at the Pyramid to the river park on boats resembling ancient Egyptian vessels for a mix of live music and holographic images."[15]

Shlenker's inability to deliver on his numerous promises led to his falling out with Tigrett. In a January 1991 letter, Tigrett wrote to Shlenker: "With much regret, I must say that if you wish to continue running the Pyramid Companies, you will have to borrow from some of your own assets for funding or find funding from other sources."[16] With none of the promised attractions in place, the Pyramid was to function solely as a basketball arena. The problem was that, apart from needing $3 million to continue running the project, Shlenker needed $5 million to fund the basketball floor, the goals, and the rims. On June 17, 1991, Shlenker's and Tigrett's contracts were terminated. The city had already moved the opening of the building from May to November. Mayor Dick Hackett lost the election to Willie Herenton partially because the Pyramid turned out to be such a disaster before it had even opened.

On November 9, 1991, the Pyramid opened with a concert by country duo the Judds, who were on a farewell tour and played for the last time in Memphis. Although the most memorable thing about the event was the flooding toilets, it was seen as rather successful, at least according to the opinions quoted in local newspapers. The positive reception of the event and the building itself led a spurned Hackett to remark on opening

Jason Williams, a player known for his creativity and flashy play, was brought in prior to the move to Memphis in order to make the Grizzlies a more captivating team.

night about his lost election: "I wish this could have opened a month ago."[17] The statement ignored the racial divisions in the city, as Herenton "failed to receive a shred of support from the white business and political establishment."[18] And yet he won, with the support of Black voters.

The first basketball game in the arena took place on November 29, 1991, with the Tigers playing against DePaul. ESPN televised the game, which took place in front of a sellout crowd of 20,142 fans. Memphis standout Anfernee Hardaway took the court for the first time for MSU during an official game. He had 18 points, 15 rebounds, six assists, four blocks, four steals, and 13 turnovers. He opened the night with 1/8 shooting. The Tigers lost 89–92 in overtime.

The university continued to use the Pyramid for basketball games and graduations, but when the NBA came around ten years later, the building was already outdated. When building the new arena was being negotiated, the county still owed $22.5 million and the city $16.5 million for construction. Those opposing the construction of a new arena on the other side of downtown Memphis preferred to just improve the existing one. According to the pursuit group, improvements would cost $192.2 million and take two years.[19] Speaking for the whole committee handling the relocation, Joel Litvin, NBA executive vice president of legal and business affairs, said: "The Pyramid is certainly an adequate temporary facility, but it's not a long-term solution."[20] The decision to relocate was hanging on the promise of a new arena being built in two to three years.

When on May 3, 2001, the Hornets decided to spend one more year in Charlotte, the decision was up to the NBA whether the Grizzlies would be allowed to move to Memphis. On the May 29, the city was visited by Commissioner Stern, the relocation committee, and league officials. The visit was clearly intended to put pressure on city officials to agree to provide most of the $250 million necessary to build the new arena. There was also a decision deadline put in place, which was two weeks. The predominant narrative was that the city not so much wanted, but needed, the NBA's approval. It already came from members of the relocation committee, who praised the City of Memphis for its developed downtown. Around the same time, public funding for the Hornets' new arena was also being voted on. The vote concerned a $342 million sports package, including $205 million for the new sports arena. Charlotte held a public referendum, and voters did not back the project, with the turn-around being around 30 percent. Memphis did not hold a referendum; the city council was tasked with the decision. By a 10–3 vote, it gave pre-liminary approval to the project and issued a $12 million appropriation for the project's start-up costs. A week later, the County Commission approved arena funding by a 10–2 vote.

There was no public referendum held on the construction of the arena, and the taxpayers were divided on the issue of public funding—especially because there was a number of conditions not only to land, but also to keep an NBA franchise. The team would already have the advantage of making more on gate receipts in Memphis than it had in Vancouver, because it would no longer have to concern itself with the Canadian–American dollar exchange rate. Heisley estimated that with the same attendance the team would make twice the money, especially since it would get almost all the profits from concessions and parking, to which it was not entitled in Vancouver.[21] The private business sector agreed to guarantee five thousand season tickets annually for the fifteen years of the arena lease.

Willie Herenton, the first elected African American mayor in the his-tory of Memphis, also got involved in the process, promising not to pay for the arena with property taxes. Holding office since 1991, the former city schools superintendent in the year 2000 vowed not to introduce new taxes for the next three years and wanted to keep that promise. The arena was to be funded by revenue bonds rather than a mixture of gen-eral obligation bonds and property tax money. The Memphis and Shelby County Sports Authority was to issue up to $230 million in bonds. A new 2 percent tax was introduced on rental cars in Shelby County as well. The state contributed $20 million for "site acquisition and infrastructure improvements."[22] The city and county were also to contribute $12 million each. Overall, the arena budget was set at $250 million, but $7 million was supposed to be spent on the improvements to the Pyramid in or-der to make it into a functional NBA arena for the next two years. Even before the details of the new arena were set, one thing was certain—it would be named after FedEx, most probably FedExForum. In October, the name was made official, the company bought the naming rights for twenty years for $90 million.

Memphis attorney Duncan Ragsdale filed a lawsuit to block construction of the arena, stating that while the decision regarding the bonds cleared the state from the responsibility of holding a referendum, it was presumed that if something went wrong or additional costs appeared, they would be handled from taxpayer money. Chancellor Walter Evans ruled in favor of Ragsdale's lawsuit, adding that the citizens of the state should get their say and at least 75 percent of the voters should approve the arena's funding plan.[23] Ragsdale said what all the other opponents of the relocation process had said: the Grizzlies already had an arena, the Pyramid, which was just ten years old. City and county officials appealed Evans's ruling, and less than a month later the ruling was overturned by the Court of Appeals. If the discussion continued, it would hurt the taxpayers even more, as the Grizzlies were to receive $3.75 million from the city if the arena was not be ready in time for the start of the 2003–04 season.

On June 23, 2001, the Grizzlies moved their basketball department to Memphis, even though the league had not yet approved the move. They selected Pau Gasol with the third overall pick and Shane Battier with the sixth overall pick from their temporary base in The Peabody Hotel. The roster being assembled was a clear indication that the Memphis Grizzlies were a different team than the Vancouver Grizzlies. Mike Bibby was traded to the Sacramento Kings with Brent Price, in exchange for Jason Williams and Nick Anderson. It was Bibby's agent, David Falk, who brokered the deal. Abdur-Rahim, the closest thing to a star the Grizzlies had up until that point, was traded to the Atlanta Hawks for the third overall pick, veteran point guard Brevin Knight and Lorenzen Wright.

Wright immediately became the most cheered for player on the team, and for good reason—he was a product of Memphis basketball. Born in Oxford, Mississippi, he played at Booker T. Washington High in Memphis, and then played for the Tigers for two seasons, before making himself eligible for the 1996 NBA Draft. The 6'11" man was selected seventh by the Clippers in one of the best drafts of all time. His inclusion in the trade was seen as something more than a move to make the salaries match in the Abdur-Rahim-for-Gasol trade. Because of his close ties with the city, Wright actually cared about the franchise finding a home in Memphis, and he best exemplified the attitude of the city: "I'm going to have bad games. But I'm going to work hard. . . . I'm going to be the guy that hustles and dives on the floor for loose balls."[24]

While Wright was sure to provide fans with an emotional connection to the team, Jason Williams was the one who undoubtedly would bring the excitement. Nicknamed "White Chocolate," the point guard was picked in the same draft as Bibby, seventh overall, losing stock for testing positive for marijuana twice in college. The way he played basketball, with flashy dribbles and passes, made every game of the season a must-watch, however, he was equally susceptible to having a bad shooting night, with more turnovers than assists. Williams was unpredictable; Bibby was stable. The Kings' best player, Chris Webber, was friends with Williams, and team owners, the Maloof family, actually treated the point guard like family, but his bad decisions cost his team numerous times. As observed by *The Californian*'s Sean Devey: "Bibby is not marketable as Williams, and the Grizzlies made the trade because they think Williams will sell tickets as the team moves to Memphis. Give credit to the Kings for sacrificing sales for wins."[25] That assumption would turn out to be accurate, as the Kings would make the Conference Finals during the following season. The Grizzlies would once again win twenty-three games.

To construct the arena, the Memphis Arena Public Building Authority picked the same company that built the Conseco Fieldhouse in Indianapolis, the league's newest arena, which was also its first retro-styled sports facility. The FedExForum was built in a bit over two years, so it met the franchise-imposed deadline and saved the city from paying a fine. Franchise executives complained about losing money during the Grizzlies' stay in the Pyramid due to the lack of luxury suites. Conseco Fieldhouse, located in downtown Indianapolis, had sixty-nine luxury suites. The demands of the Memphis investment group and the owner were that the new arena have 18,500 seats, including twenty-five hundred club seats, seventy-five luxury suites, and a parking garage with at least eighteen hundred spaces.[26] The arena was to be built on the south side of Beale Street, and it was expected that its appearance would match the surroundings, plus bring in tourists visiting the city to attend Grizzlies' games.

The new arena was designed by architectural firm Ellerbe Becket out of Kansas City, Missouri. The groundbreaking ceremony took place on June 20, 2002. It was estimated that up to three thousand people came to the ceremony despite bad weather. There were speeches by Mayor Herenton and Mayor Rout as well as a musical performance by local soul singer David Porter. At the end, attendants were encouraged to collect the dirt into special souvenir jars with the words "I Dug It" written on them.[27] The franchise was represented by the dance team and the team mascot as well as by an important member of the front office, Jerry West, who added legitimacy to the franchise, just as the NBA team was supposed to add legitimacy to the city.

West was a star player and executive for the Los Angeles Lakers, winning eight NBA Championships for the organization (although only one as a player). He treated the Grizzlies as a challenge and the promising core of rookies Pau Gasol (2002 Rookie of the Year) and Shane Battier as well as point guard Jason Williams already made for a solid foundation. West spoke of the Grizzlies winning the NBA Championship somewhere in the future as possibly the greatest thrill of his life. He described being the underdog as "fun" and spoke of targeting players who wanted to be part of the community, who would come to Memphis not just to play basketball. John Calipari, who had previously dealt with West in the NBA, as coach and executive vice president of the New Jersey Nets, had nothing but praise for the new Grizzlies' president of basketball operations, adding: "What he has done in the NBA, building the Lakers, he did it with super picks. He found diamonds in the rough, and then he swung some big trades."[28] With the fourth pick in the draft, West chose power forward Drew Gooden, even though the team already had Gasol, Wright, and Stromile Swift as potential starting players. He signed and traded, and as a result the Grizzlies entered training camp with twenty players, eleven being newcomers. Coach Sidney Lowe had no doubt that the franchise would finally overcome its record of twenty-three wins: "No question, we'll be better. We just have to stay healthy."[29]

The Grizzlies started the 2002–03 season 0–8, and Lowe resigned. He was replaced by veteran coach Hubie Brown, whose last coaching job had been in 1986, when he was fired by the New York Knicks after a 4–12 start. Fifty-three years old at the time, Brown returned to coaching as a sixty-nine-year-old. For years, his name was thrown around in rumors, but up until that point he continued to hold on to his position as tv analyst and commentator. George Karl and Pat Riley, both successful NBA coaches, compared Brown's return to the league to that of NFL's Dick Vermeil, who left the Philadelphia Eagles in 1982 and returned to coach the St. Louis Rams in 1997, at age sixty-two. Two years later, the Rams won the Super Bowl. Brown was hired to develop the young Memphis roster and serve as a teacher. Upon meeting the players, he immediately informed them that it was "his way or the highway."[30] Under Brown, the Grizzlies went 28–46, finally beating the shameful record of twenty-three wins during a season. What makes their regular season record from 2002–03 all the more impressive is that they lost the first five games of Brown's tenure as well, starting the season 0–13.

Construction of the roster was going much like the construction of the FedExForum, which on July 22, 2003, was heavily affected by a windstorm, which damaged three cranes and caused $1.2 million in losses. The storm also forced Beale Street to temporarily close, impacting the city's tourist revenue as well. The costs were not covered by insurance, so the city and county were tasked with making up for the deficit. The FedExForum events were supposed to generate $1.15 per ticket for the city, but the arena needed to be complete first. In the meantime, the Grizzlies continued to play in the Pyramid, where they were near the bottom of the league in attendance. After ten years, the arena was already outdated, with tight seating and a lack of basic accommodations.

In the second season of the Brown-West partnership, the third-youngest roster in the NBA finally got on the right track. And it was not that the team improved gradually. The Grizzlies made the leap from twenty-eight to fifty wins in less than a year, and earned their first playoff appearance. Brown introduced defensive strategies and teamwork, using a ten-man rotation. Originally the decision to play so many players was meant to develop as many of them as possible. Brown explained the approach as follows: "The worst thing for young players is they come in and they play 22 minutes tonight. The next game they don't even get in."[31] He made it his priority to talk to every player after every game and patiently explain why things went the way they did. Ten players averaged at least nineteen minutes per game and five averaged double-figures in points. Brown was named Coach of the Year, while West won Executive of the Year for the second time in their careers. Brown won the trophy for the first time in 1978, as the head coach of the Hawks; West won it in 1995 with the Lakers. Memphis suddenly had a successful, respectable team on its hands. It did not matter that the young Grizzlies were swept by the Spurs in the first round of the playoffs. There was no shame in losing to the reigning NBA Champions.

The leap came just in time for the opening of the new arena, which was supposed to represent the whole city. General contractor M.A. Mortenson Co. gave 27.8 percent of construction contracts to minority- and women-owned businesses. This meant $41 million in construction contracts given to minority- and women-owned firms and $26 million in construction contracts for Black-owned firms.[32] However, part of the deal according to which Grizzlies owned the arena was that they held the noncompete clause, which successfully limited work in other venues. On September 6, the FedExForum held an open house event among protests from independent contractors who worked basketball games in the Pyramid. Crew One Productions, the company tasked with hiring the contractors, offered less money than Local 69, who worked in the Pyramid and paid the workers better wages.

In the main narrative, that was just a minor storyline. What was more important was that the Grizzlies would share the new arena with the University of Memphis Tigers, who signed a twenty-year lease with the FedExForum. The negotiations went on for two years and, according to the terms of the deal, the Tigers were to annually receive $800,000 from the Grizzlies, $125,000 from the City Council, and $125,000 from the Shelby County Commission. The payment from the franchise was to be reduced accordingly if game-attendance fell below ten thousand. Mayor Herenton originally proposed $4.5 million worth of improvements to make the Tigers stay at the Pyramid, but a week later pushed for a deal between the Grizzlies and the Tigers, convinced to change his mind by the above-mentioned numbers.[33] Meanwhile, despite housing two

Hubie Brown took over the Grizzlies when he was sixty-nine years old, and in only his second season he was named Coach of the Year after taking the young roster to the playoffs.

basketball teams, the Pyramid was losing up to $1.5 million per year. The guaranteed payment made more sense for the university, even though it had to sacrifice its scheduling and naming rights in the process.

The first gala held in the FedExForum was the opening of Memphis Rock 'n' Soul Museum, which was moved there from the nearby Gibson Guitar factory. Around one thousand guests took part in the event, so it was not a real test for the building. Originally the arena was one of the venues considered for hosting the MTV Video Music Awards, but eventually it opened with a sold-out concert of Tennessee-raised R&B singer Usher, attended by 14,131 fans. The first sporting event held in the FedExForum was a boxing gala consisting of thirteen matches, and headlined by the IBF light heavyweight title bout between Glen Johnson and Roy Jones Jr. The main event of the evening disappointed, as Jones was knocked out after just forty-eight seconds, but all in all the gala was still considered a success, largely because of the atmosphere in the arena.

For the Grizzlies, it would hopefully become a vital recruiting tool for free agents, who simply did not want to sign with the team back in Vancouver. West had high hopes for the FedExForum, stating: "This will be a building that allows us to continue to build this to hopefully a championship-caliber team."[34] If that were to happen, it would be without coach Brown. While the seventy-one-year-old was medically cleared to continue work as head coach, after twelve games and the team going 5–7, Brown retired, citing "unexpected health-related issues," which were "unforeseen and absolutely nonexistent at the beginning of the season."[35] He claimed that he lacked the drive and passion on a day-to-day basis. His overall record on the Grizzlies was 83–85, by far the best in the franchise's short history.

The Grizzlies brought back the same ten-man rotation, which turned out to be a problem. Already at the end of the previous season, Jerry West praised the coach for hiding the team's "weaknesses all year long," adding that with the Grizzlies being last in the league in defensive rebounds, he would make sure to bring in a big man.[36] No such trade was made, and the only significant change was releasing fan-favorite role player Bo Outlaw. He appeared in all eighty-two games in 2003–04, started just one, and was making around two shots per game, but he fought for every ball and was a ferocious rebounder and defender. In a couple of years, players like him would come to define professional basketball in Memphis.

The Grizzlies were playing their season opener at home, against the Washington Wizards. The Wizards won just twenty-five games in 2003–04 and had not made the playoffs since 1996–97, which was their last season as the Bullets. But they were about to turn things around and make the playoffs four seasons in a row. Despite missing three of their starters, they won against the favored Grizzlies. Soon, tensions within the roster started mounting. Jason Williams, Bonzi Wells, and James Posey were no longer happy sharing their minutes with other players. It was later revealed that Brown asked management to trade the three disgruntled players, and when that did not happen, he wanted to put them on the injured list. Jason Williams got in a heated argument with Brown's son, Brendan, who was the team's assistant coach, responsible for offensive play-calling, during the third quarter of the third game of the 2004–05 season. Williams, Wells, and Posey were traded after the season concluded. Once they were gone, *The Commercial Appeal's* Ronald Tillery said that, apart from getting physically ill, Brown "got sick of the insubordination, disrespect and gutless behavior that started with Williams and ended with [his] abrupt resignation."[37]

Brown was replaced by another coach working a long time as a broadcaster, defensive specialist Mike Fratello, after a 0–4 transition period under interim coach Lionel Hollins. The 1986 Coach of the Year with the Atlanta Hawks, Fratello also coached the Cleveland Cavaliers of the late 1990s, who became notorious for their slow pace and low scoring. Like Brown, the fifty-seven-year-old was a strict disciplinarian. He almost immediately started clashing with Williams, who was not as flashy as in earlier years, as he had changed his style due to the number of turnovers he was averaging. In his first season in Memphis, he was averaging 3.3 turnovers per game, which was close to his three-per-game average in Sacramento. In his last two seasons on the Grizzlies, he was averaging less than two. He was, however, still prone to making bad decisions and grew frustrated with Fratello, complaining about playing time, even one time calling his coach a "bitch."[38] After the Grizzlies were eliminated from the 2005 playoffs in a first-round sweep by the Suns, Williams started yelling at *The Commercial Appeal's* Geoff Calkins when the columnist was interviewing Grizzlies' players. Williams twice took Calkins' pen and eventually had to be taken out of the team locker room. The point guard was fined $10,000. After the 2004–05 season, he was traded, along with Posey, to the Heat. Alongside Shaquille O'Neal and Dwyane Wade, they would win the 2006 NBA Championship.

Jerry West did not fulfill his dream of building a championship contender from the ground up. By the end of his contract, he announced that he was not going to renew it. The Grizzlies finished the 2006–07 season with twenty-two wins, the worst record in the NBA. The team was in need of a rebuild, and the sixty-nine-year-old did not have the time, or the energy, to go through one. With Pau Gasol (first All-Star in franchise history in 2006) and Mike Miller (2006 Sixth Man of the Year) left from the most successful period in franchise history, and Shane Battier traded for rookie swingman Rudy Gay, West was willing to step down and pass the reins to Chris Wallace as both general manager and vice president of basketball operations.

Wallace had experience as director of player personnel for the Miami Heat and general manager of the Boston Celtics. In his two years in Miami, he discovered two important members of the Heat rotation, Isaac Austin and Voshon Lenard, who helped the Heat win a franchise-record sixty-one games in the 1996–97 season. Earlier, he worked as a scout and talent evaluator for the Blazers, the Nuggets, the Clippers, and the Knicks. When announcing his resignation, West also hinted as to why he failed to bring a title to Memphis: "There's been a lot of turmoil here. The ownership thing have made it very difficult to concentrate on what we need to do here to improve our basketball team."[39]

Chapter 7

Grit & Grind

Fratello was fired after the Grizzlies went 6–24 since the start of the 2005–06 season, but he was still the winningest coach in franchise history, with ninety-five wins and eighty-three losses, and the only one with a positive win-loss ratio. The team was last in the league in attendance. In fact, for the next four seasons, the Grizzlies would never rank higher than twenty-seventh out of thirty teams. In this trying moment, Heisley once again announced his intention to sell the franchise. The process of looking for a potential owner had secretly been going on for about a year. It was believed that he wanted to do sell while the team still had its biggest asset, Jerry West, whose contract would be over in the summer of 2007.[1] In order for the new owner not to inherit one of the highest payrolls in the league, West was tasked with making trades that would keep the roster salaries under the luxury tax.

On October 2, 2006, the potential new owner was announced. During a hastily organized press conference, Heisley handed the Grizzlies uniform to a thirty-six-year-old former Duke player, Brian Keith Davis. The two reached a deal according to which the Davis-led group, including his Duke teammate and recently retired NBA veteran Christian Laettner, would pay 70 percent of the $360 million that the Grizzlies were worth to Heisley, which amounted to $252 million in total. The local minority owners had sixty days to match the offer, but it was almost certain that they would not be able to come up with that kind of money. There was a lot of justifiable doubt that Davis was capable of coming up with that type of money either, but he made the impression that he could get things done. As a teenager, he climbed his way to Duke men's basketball team's roster, and while in college continued to intern at various companies every year during summer break. Davis had close connections in the league after a two-year internship in the NBA's New York offices.

During the conference, Davis proclaimed that Jerry West, the best-paid executive in the league, could get a lifetime contract with the Grizzlies if he wanted to. He added that Laettner would unretire and continue his thirteen-year NBA career on the Grizzlies, but soon backed out of that statement. Davis was secretive about the rest of the investment group, but said that they were "the biggest players in the world," adding: "we'll have an NFL guy and we'll have a Hollywood guy. How about that? The Hollywood guy's probably more famous than the NFL guy, but you guys will know him."[2]

Heisley was so confident in the bid coming to fruition that he moved away from the franchise and retreated to St. Charles, Illinois, where he resided for most of the year. On December 1, 2006, the Memphis ownership group officially announced it had no intentions of matching the offer. The same day, Davis and Laettner, who were met with significant skepticism by the city, announced that just as they had redeveloped Durham, North Carolina, they would do so on a much larger scale in Memphis. The citizens of Tennessee, parts of which once formed the buckle of the Bible Belt, were partially distrustful of the two due to Laettner's late-career suspension for marijuana use. Davis was not a local, just like Heisley, but he promised to move his family to Memphis following the acquisition.

In 1995 Davis, Laettner and developer Tom Niemann had formed Blue Devil Ventures, a development company, named after their Duke connection. A year later, they bought five old tobacco warehouses in downtown Durham for $2.2 million and turned them into West Village, an apartment complex with commercial space. They proved that they could get investors on board and bring their projects to fruition. It was only later that their business endeavors failed and Laettner was forced to file for bankruptcy; in hindsight, not buying the franchise actually saved it. They had until January 15, 2007, to buy the team, but on December 5, 2006, NBA officials already announced that the Grizzlies were not for sale, as the proposed buyers did not provide information on who would be responsible for financing the sale. Davis himself was planning to invest between $40 million and $55 million of his own money.[3]

Former NCAA legend Christian Laettner was close to becoming the co-owner of the Grizzlies in 2007.

By January 15, 2007, Davis and Laettner became owners of a professional sports team, but it was not the Grizzlies. They acquired operating rights to DC United, a Washington-based MLS franchise, for $33 million. One move did not have to exclude the other, but the expected date passed and no offer for the Grizzlies appeared. Heisley was still looking for potential buyers, washing his hands of the eventual relocation, saying: "Mike Heisley is not moving this team. If I sell it to somebody, and they move it, I have no control over that."[4] He expected potential offers to be around $350 million. The local ownership group wanted to buy him out and initially offered $250 million. The situation remained the same, Heisley was still the owner. Then they offered $300 million, and he once again turned them down.

In January 2007, West and Heisley made an attempt to trade their only star, Pau Gasol, to the Chicago Bulls, but the team from Illinois was not willing to part with two out of three of their best players: Luol Deng, Ben Gordon, and Kirk Hinrich. The Nets wanted to exchange Gasol for Vince Carter, the man partially responsible for saving NBA basketball in Canada. Carter, however, was no longer capable of being the best player on a winning team. Apart from the ownership situation, the play of the Grizzlies also alienated their fanbase, as Gasol was considered "too soft" to be the number one option on an NBA team. He was criticized for his lack of rebounds and defense, despite having career-best averages of 9.8 rebounds and 2.1 blocks during the 2006–07 season. Gasol himself felt "betrayed" because he did not want to be traded, but wanted to be a part of a winning team.[5] With the Grizzlies in for a rebuild, he had no chance of winning in Memphis anytime soon.

Preaching patience, the team hired longtime NBA assistant Marc Iavaroni to be head coach, passing on more experienced and bigger names, like Larry Brown and Kiki Vandeweghe, who interviewed for the job as well. Iavaroni wanted to implement the style of basketball that was so successful on the last team he was on, the Phoenix Suns. Led by Steve Nash, the Suns made two Western Conference Finals in a row and were seen as a team of the future, playing fast-paced, finesse basketball. Nash was the mastermind behind that offense, proving that in order to work, that system needed a pass-first point guard. Pau Gasol and the newly signed center Darko Milicic, who could play both inside and outside, were perfect for that system. Milicic was slowly rebuilding his reputation in the league, and was now on pace to be considered a functional role player rather than a draft bust, selected in front of Carmelo Anthony, Chris Bosh, and Dwyane Wade. If the Grizzlies did not trade what became their 2003 pick to the Pistons in 1997 for Otis Thorpe, Milicic's career could have played out very differently. Signing with the Grizzlies was his chance at redemption.

In the 2007 draft lottery, the Grizzlies once again were unlucky and landed the fourth pick, even though they were the worst team in the league. They selected Mike Conley, this time their actual point guard of the future, one of the cornerstones of the "Grit & Grind" Grizzlies. In the same draft, with the forty-eighth pick, the Los Angeles Lakers selected Marc Gasol, who would become another important part of the "new" Grizzlies. On February 1, 2008, the Memphis team acquired the rights to the younger Gasol brother (who was playing his final season in Girona, Spain), as well as 2008 and 2010 Lakers' first-round draft picks, Kwame Brown, Javaris Crittenton, and Aaron McKie, for Marc's older brother, Pau.

For years, moving the best player in franchise history to the Lakers was considered one of the worst trades in NBA history. It has been assumed that Heisley forced the new general manager, Chris Wallace, to make the deal in order to free up cap space, as Gasol had three years left on his contract. San Antonio Spurs coach Gregg Popovich was very critical of the trade, saying before a game: "What they did in Memphis is beyond comprehension. There should be a trade committee that can scratch all trades that make no sense. I just wish I had been on a trade committee that oversees NBA trades. I'd like to elect myself to that committee. I would have voted no to the L.A. trade."[6] Heisley himself defended the trade, as if it would be something wanted by the community, with whom Gasol supposedly fell out of favor.[7] Wallace estimated that, thanks to the move in the summer of 2009, the Grizzlies would free up to $17 million in cap space.[8] That reasoning was questionable, as the franchise had almost no luck signing free agents.

In fact, Milicic might have been the biggest name signed by the Grizzlies up to that point. Having him on the roster alongside Kwame

Brown, who was also considered one of the biggest busts in NBA history, made the franchise the subject of ridicule. It was clear that the Grizzlies had no intentions of being good that season. They won just twenty-two games, were third from the bottom, and ended up with the fifth overall pick. They picked power forward Kevin Love out of UCLA, who was precisely the player they needed during the Gasol years. After making the selection, Wallace described him as "a rebounder, tremendous passer. . . . He may be the best outlet passer in the game of basketball."[9]

The next day, as the second round of the draft was underway, Wallace traded Love to the Timberwolves for the third pick, O. J. Mayo. Six other players were involved in the move, the most important being Mike Miller, who grew really close with the Memphis community. Originally, the Grizzlies wanted to move up in the draft to select Michael Beasley with the second overall pick, but the Miami Heat, who were holding the selection, were willing to part with it only in exchange for Rudy Gay. Beasley would have a rather disappointing NBA career, especially since future All-NBA players, Russell Westbrook and Kevin Love, were picked almost immediately after him.

If the Grizzlies had the first pick, they would undoubtedly select point guard Derrick Rose, who attended University of Memphis. He joined the program because of Coach Calipari's ability to get players into the NBA as well as the possibility of being mentored by Rod Strickland, a once-great point guard, who was now a member of the Tigers' staff. Strickland called Rose "a throwback . . . a pass-first point guard who is explosive enough to score."[10] Rose, who lived his whole life in Chicago until his move to Memphis, was the focal point of a team that lost just two games during the 2007–08 season. Unfortunately, one of these games was the NCAA Final, in which they fell in overtime to Kansas. If Memphis landed the first pick, his stay would make for a captivating narrative, but once it was announced that the Bulls were picking first, the story of the prodigal son returning to bring the title to his hometown franchise made for an even better story—one that could be properly marketed and monetized, with Chicago being a big market city.

Mayo was supposed to make up for the loss of Miller, as he was capable of similar shooting, but played better defense. With Conley, Mayo, and Gay, the Grizzlies had one of the more promising backcourts in the league. Gay came in second in Most Improved Player voting for his second NBA season, improving his scoring average from 10.8 to 20.1 points per game. The trio was joined by rookies Darrell Arthur (picked twenty-seventh in 2008) and Marc Gasol (who decided to enter the NBA at age twenty-four) in the frontcourt, becoming the youngest and least-experienced starting five in the NBA. The last team that relied so heavily on rookies, the 1997–98 Denver Nuggets, had two rookies (point guard Bobby Jackson and power forward/center Tony Battie) in the starting lineup, and a third one starting twenty-three games (power forward Danny Fortson). They won only eleven games.

In her 2009 book on the globalization processes taking place in Memphis, Wanda Rushing describes the Grizzlies as a disappointment and the possibility of the franchise leaving the city as increasing.[11] This skepticism toward the Grizzlies would soon change—and the exact moment in which the mood shifted is described in the chapter on Zach Randolph and Bryant Reeves, "Two Fifties." The young Grizzlies managed to win twenty-four games in 2008–09, including eleven under their new coach, Lionel Hollins.

Hollins was the point guard on the 1977 NBA Champions, the Portland Trail Blazers. He played for the team for five seasons and was partially responsible for Blazermania, the craze that swept through Portland, with the whole city almost unanimously supporting the team. Hollins's number 14 jersey was retired by the Blazers on April 18, 2007. Greg Jayne of Vancouver's *The Columbian* wrote that, by retiring Hollins's number—along with those of fellow Blazers Dave Twardzik, Lloyd Neal, and Larry Steele, as part of celebrating thirty years of the only championship in franchise history—"Portland is reinforcing its image as a second-rate franchise content to feast on the residue of its lone championship."[12] The assessment had little value, as it was coming from the inhabitant of a city that failed to produce a winning NBA franchise, let alone keep it for as long as Portland had.

After retiring in 1985, Hollins became the assistant coach for his alma mater, Arizona State, working there during the 1985–86 and 1987–88 seasons. He finished his degree, and at age thirty-four, joined the coaching staff of the Phoenix Suns. Hollins preferred to work in the NBA rather than recruit prospects for the ASU program, as he wanted to work on pure basketball skills rather than teach, instruct, and mentor young talent.[13] In 1995, he left Phoenix for Vancouver, joining the staff of the upstart Grizzlies. After one season in Canada, he applied for the head-coaching position on the Sixers, but was passed over in favor of his teammate on that championship Blazers team, Johnny Davis. Davis lasted just one year in Philadelphia, a team overrun with strong personalities like Allen Iverson, Jerry Stackhouse, and Derrick Coleman. After getting another shot at being a head coach, this time on the Magic, Davis bounced around as an assistant, working on the Timberwolves and the Pacers, before joining the Grizzlies in 2007. There, he replaced Hollins, who was yet to get a shot at being officially named the head coach in the NBA, but managed to land two interim stints with the Grizzlies, first in 1999, while the team was still in Vancouver, and then in 2004, in Memphis.

After working for eleven years with the Grizzlies, including six years in British Columbia, Hollins found himself without a job after the 2006–07 season, as Iavaroni no longer wanted him on his staff. The coach took a year off, but stayed in Memphis, teaching basketball and leadership at the Grizzlies Academy. Hollins loved working for the Memphis community, and said the occupation gave him the freedom to do what he wanted, plus provided him with a reason to wake up in the morning.[14] Still, once the new season came around, he was once again on the coaching staff, albeit of a different team, the Milwaukee Bucks, serving as an assistant under head coach Scott Skiles.

Meanwhile Davis was the assistant under Iavaroni, whose team began the season on a good foot, but then lost fifteen out of seventeen games and after the 11–30 record during the season (33-90 overall), Iavaroni was dismissed. Iavaroni's up-tempo style was not particularly successful in Bluff City. At the time of his firing, the team was twenty-ninth in the league in scoring. Davis became the interim coach for four games, all of which the Grizzlies lost all four. Meanwhile, Wallace was negotiating with Hollins. The coach was a man of principle, who always stuck to his beliefs, and for him that was what made him a true winner. Hollins was concerned with the down mood on the team and asked his mentor, Doug Allred, who coached him in junior high, for advice. Allred said: "Embrace them and love them and rejoice in their abilities."[15] He followed the advice, but it would take the City of Memphis some time to listen to it as well. In the next two seasons, despite winning forty and forty-six games, respectively, the Grizzlies were twenty-seventh in attendance. Next season though, 2011–12, they made the leap to twentieth. The team was riding the momentum of the 2011 postseason run, which stopped just one win shy of the Western Conference Finals.

The final piece of the roster came in 2010, when defensive-minded shooting guard, Tony Allen, signed with the Grizzlies for three years and $9.4 million. The Chicago native was picked twenty-fifth in the 2004 NBA Draft by the Celtics. Even before Allen played in the NBA, Celtics' coach Doc Rivers praised the player for his toughness and ability to get to the basket.[16] While in college, he was most famous for becoming the first player in Oklahoma State history to score over one thousand points in just two seasons. In his early NBA career, Allen was a slasher, able to easily find his way to the basket. In the summer of 2007, he was one of the few players the Celtics retained when making the moves that brought them Ray Allen and Kevin Garnett. During the team's 2008 championship playoff run, Allen appeared in fifteen games for a total of sixty-five minutes. The team was planning to move on from him in the summer. Not only did the Celtics not bother to make him a restricted free agent by extending a qualifying offer, but they also drafted a similar player in J. R. Giddens. Once it turned out that swingman James Posey was leaving, Allen was re-signed.

After two more years in Boston, providing relief for Rajon Rondo, Ray Allen, and Paul Pierce, as well as playing solid defense, Tony Allen was again a free agent. The Celtics re-signed Ray Allen and Pierce, and signed center Jermaine O'Neal. Tony Allen was waiting for a three-year guaranteed deal, the Celtics were only willing to give him a two-year contract. The Celtics were over the salary cap and could retain Allen without cap constraints. Still, they preferred to wait and, as a consequence, the Grizzlies gained a player who would soon earn the nickname "the Grindfather."

Allen truly embraced the Grit & Grind mentality. He would even give that name to his charity. Allen, Conley, Gasol, and Randolph formed the core of the Grit & Grind Grizzlies, also known as The Core Four. Other members of the roster, like Gay, Mayo, Tayshaun Prince, Mike

Miller, Vince Carter, Jeff Green, or Matt Barnes, remained interchange-able. They even switched coaches, from Hollins to Dave Joerger, but they always remained the Grit & Grind Grizzlies, and played the same brand of slow-paced, defensive-minded basketball. From 2011 to 2017, they fought in the postseason against flashy and explosive Thunder, the "Lob City" Clippers, the perfectly organized Spurs, and the seemingly unstoppable Warriors. They were never the favorites, and sometimes they won, sometimes they lost, but they had the support of the city throughout. When Heisley was approached in the summer of 2012 by California billionaire Larry Ellison about selling the franchise, the owner refused, stating: "We're not even considering [him], this team cannot be moved."[17] Ellison wanted to buy the franchise and move it to California, following his failed bid to buy the Golden State Warriors in 2010.

The same year Heisley sold the Grizzlies to another California busi-nessman, the thirty-four-year-old Robert J. Pera, who paid $377 million for the franchise. On June 11, 2012, Pera submitted a $10 million deposit. He also guaranteed that the franchise would stay in Memphis for the next fifteen years. Lionel Hollins went through three ownership changes as head/interim coach, and each one was followed by him getting de-moted or fired. Upon the announcement of the change in ownership, Gasol hoped that the team could maintain direction and keep the same staff, saying: "None of this would have been possible without Coach. He completely changed the mentality of the team. Everything starts with Coach. I don't see this team without Coach."[18]

The Grizzlies entered the 2012–13 season with a new owner, who came with his own ideas about running the franchise. Pera brought in Sixers minority shareholder Jason Levien to be the team's CEO and hired *ESPN* writer John Hollinger as vice president of basketball operations. The NBA was on the cusp of the analytics revolution, and Hollinger wanted the team to rely more on advanced statistics. He even traded the best scorer on the roster, Rudy Gay, because the data showed that the team would play better without him. And he was right, as the Grizzlies made the Western Conference Finals for the first time in their history that same season. An old school coach, Hollins was reluctant to implement data into his game schemes. The tensions had been going on throughout the 2012–13 season, and when Gay was traded, Hollins openly criticized

Pau Gasol really wanted to stay in Memphis, but his trade to the Lakers brought in his younger brother, Marc, who became an important part of the "Grit & Grind" Grizzlies.

the move, even talked about leaving the team after the season. When during a postseason practice session Hollinger entered the court and started instructing one of the players, the executive and Hollins got into an argument. The philosophical differences regarding the game of basketball were too big to overcome. Hollins's contract was not renewed, and his assistant, Dave Joerger, was named the new head coach.

The Grizzlies had a hip new owner, stability, were following the newest trends, and remained competitive up until the 2017 playoffs. After falling to the Spurs in the first round, the roster was dismantled. Both Allen and Randolph left in free agency. The team then began a rebuild, in the process of which both Marc Gasol and Mike Conley were traded away. Conley was traded to the Jazz before the 2019–20 season, while Gasol left for the Toronto Raptors earlier in the year in a mid-season trade. The Raptors, the sole Canadian team in the NBA, celebrated their first championship in 2019, with Gasol as its starting center.

The title did not go unnoticed in Vancouver. On October 17, 2019, in Rogers Arena—as the former GM Place was now known—a preseason game took place between the Dallas Mavericks and the Los Angeles Clippers. Some fans turned out to see the dazzling European prospect, Luka Doncic, play for the Mavericks. Others showed up to see the man instrumental in bringing the first NBA Championship to Canada, Kawhi Leonard, on his new team—Leonard signed with the Clippers during the summer. The loudest voices, though, belonged to the fans who showed up in Vancouver Grizzlies jerseys and caps; 17,204 fans, two thousand from reaching the arena's capacity, chanted: "We want the Grizzlies" during the fourth quarter. Then they did it again.[19] This served as proof that people in Vancouver still remember and care for the franchise. They are still passionate about the Grizzlies and willing to support them. There are just not enough of them for the NBA to consider making a return to British Columbia.

Conclusion

In comparing the Vancouver and Memphis Grizzlies, in particular their first years in each city, I hope the reader has gained an appreciation for how complicated it can be for cities to acquire, manage, and retain a professional sports franchise. There is always a certain unpredictability local boosters must factor in when trying to lure a major league team. This prospect can become a subject of frustration and tension within a community, or can bring it together in times of crisis. With this book, I wanted to add another position to the rather scarce scholarship on franchise relocation. In *Gaming the World: How Sports Are Reshaping Global Politics and Culture*, Andrei S. Markovits and Lars Renmann write that "NBA's global presence with stars such as Michael Jordan, Magic Johnson, LeBron James, and Kobe Bryant has helped solidify the legitimacy, attractiveness, and acceptance of African Americans . . . as public figures in the white-dominated societies and cultures of Europe and America."[1] The process indeed succeeded in Canada, as proven by the influx of Canadian-born players into the NBA, including two African Canadians being selected with the first overall picks in 2013 and 2014 NBA Drafts.

While image-wise, the Vancouver Grizzlies could have been a success, their failure provided the league a valuable lesson on expansion. Apart from a quality product, which is all too often a matter of luck—as proven by the different fates of the Grizzlies and the Raptors, and the players that they drafted (not) panning out—the Grizzlies management and ownership did not put forth enough effort to market the franchise to the people of Vancouver. The forward-thinking city could indeed embrace them if the market were properly analyzed and recognized beforehand. The

Raptors, just like the Grizzlies, paid player and staff salaries in US dollars, and their ticket revenue was in Canadian dollars, which negatively impacted the earnings of both franchises. But Toronto stood behind its franchise even after Vince Carter—originally responsible for putting the franchise on the global map with his flashy plays—was traded. In fact, the fans sided with the franchise rather than with the disgruntled superstar during the conflict that led to Carter's departure.

In Vancouver, the team's struggles were seen as signs of futility and led to disappointment. In Memphis, the scrappy, slow-paced basketball was seen as an expression of the city's tenacity, its willingness to fight, to overcome crisis after crisis. Initially, the franchise was accused of fabricating "feelings of excitement and authenticity" through "appropriation of song titles to promote the Grizzlies and the FedEx Forum," as pointed out by Rushing.[2] The Grizzlies in British Columbia would be successful as a gentrified, clean-cut, and enjoyable team. In Memphis, fans cheered on when "Whoop That Trick" blasted from the speakers, just as they did after every hustle play by their team. The two cities might have been at some points NBA-franchise hungry, but satisfying that hunger required the right team. And in the Grit & Grind Grizzlies, Memphis managed to find just that.

As the roster dissolved and the franchise players left, the Grizzlies immediately lucked out in the 2019 NBA Draft in which they received the second pick, despite finishing the season 22nd in the league. Numerous teams were "tanking" or playing poorly in order to lose games and gain the possibility of landing the number one selection. In 2019 the number one selection likely meant the right to pick Zion Williamson, a physically imposing and agile power forward that was seen as a consensus franchise changer. Picking first, the Grizzlies would *have to* take Williamson, as any other decision would be universally panned. However, the first selection went to the New Orleans Pelicans, who had the same (33–49) record in the 2018–19 regular season as the Grizzlies. Coming so close to landing a generational talent could have been reminiscent of the 2003 draft lottery, when the Grizzlies landed the second pick, missing out on superstar LeBron James and relinquishing their pick to the Detroit Pistons as part of a lingering, disastrous 1997 trade for Otis Thorpe when the franchise was still in Vancouver.

This time, however, there was a generational talent was still available to them and no original sin to suffer from. With the second pick the Grizzlies selected Ja Morant, a twenty-year-old born and raised in South Carolina. Morant had gained notoriety as a high-scoring point guard who played college ball at Murray State University in southwestern Kentucky. Morant moved his family with him to Memphis so that they would handle the day-to-day aspects of life, allowing him to focus on basketball. He was quick to notice he needed assistance, by saying to his father before draft night: "I don't know how to run no house."[3] Before the family moved, Morant's father, who was a barber in the same barbershop for over two decades, gave one final haircut to his son at the family shop. The small, symbolic gesture spoke volumes about who the Morants were and what values they held as a family. They immediately made their presence felt in Memphis by collectively attending the rookie's games and being "on a first-name basis with ushers and longtime fans alike."[4]

Unfortunately, despite Morant's promise, he was still a rookie floor general, and with another rookie, Taylor Jenkins, as head coach the Grizzlies managed to win just one more game than the season prior. However, Morant's athletic dunks and incredible play soon made FedEx Forum an entertaining venue despite the team's losses. In Morant's second season the Grizzlies improved from twenty-sixth to eleventh in attendance. Earning comparisons to LeBron James's impact on the popularity of the Cavaliers and Kevin Durant's ability to set an identity for the Oklahoma City Thunder, Memphis Tourism CEO and president Kevin Kane saw Morant as able to generate millions for the community.[5] Prior to the 2022–23 season, following a playoff run cut short by an injury to Morant, ESPN decided to put 18 of the Grizzlies' games on national television—a franchise record. During the season Nike released Morant's first signature shoe, which proved that despite playing in a small market he was able to get business opportunities which he would get in other cities as well. With a fresh spotlight on Morant and the Grizzlies, the future of the team seems bright, but it remains to be seen how the city will benefit from and focus the attention.

There is no natural reason for grizzlies to be in Tennessee, so it fits that the Memphis Grizzlies seem like such fantastical creatures. But sports tend to let in the unreal, impossible, and unexpected more readily than normal life. So, in spite of the team crumbling in the 2023 playoffs and the numerous incidents on and off the court, I remain, like the weariless fans of Vancouver, ardently hopeful. That hope is why I have not written this book as a cautionary tale, but as a prelude to the great things that will eventually befall this team. If there is one NBA franchise deserving of such hope, and one fan base owed its day in the sun, it is this one.

Notes

Introduction

1. Lance Berelowitz, *Dream City: Vancouver and the Global Imagination* (Vancouver: Douglas & McIntyre, 2005), 14.

2. Yago Colas, *Ball Don't Lie!: Myth, Genealogy, and Invention in the Cultures of Basketball* (Philadelphia, PA: Temple University Press, 2016), 95.

3. James Naismith, *The James Naismith Reader: Basketball in His Own Words*, ed. Douglas Stark (Lincoln: University of Nebraska Press, 2021), 68.

4. Mark Heisler, "The Only Thing Grizzlies Succeeded at Was Failing," *The Los Angeles Times*, March 18, 2001, B7.

5. Gary Whannel, *Media Sport Stars: Masculinities and Moralities* (London: Routledge, 2002), 3.

6. Joe Kennedy, *Games without Frontiers* (London, Repeater, 2016), 31.

7. Ibid., 36.

8. Erin C. Tarver, *The I in Team: Sports Fandom and the Reproduction of Identity* (Chicago: The University of Chicago Press, 2017), 25.

9. Ibid., 20.

10. Zygmunt Baumann, *Liquid Modernity* (London: Polity, 2020), 147.

Chapter 1

1. David Swindell and Mark S. Rosentraub, "Who Benefits from the Presence of Professional Sports Teams? The Implications for Funding of Stadiums and Arenas," *Public Administration Review* 58, no. 1 (Jan–Feb, 1998): 19.

2. Arthur Schlesinger Jr., "New Mood in Politics," in *The Sixties: Art, Politics, and Media of Our Most Explosive Decade*, ed. Gerald Howard (St. Paul, MN: Paragon House, 1991), 45.

3. John F. Kennedy, "The Soft American," *Sports Illustrated*, December 26, 1960, 16.

4. Tom Wells, "Running Battle: Washington's War at Home," in *Long Time Gone: Sixties America Then and Now,* ed. by Alexander Bloom (Oxford: Oxford University Press, 2001), 83.

5. Pat Pickens, *The Whalers: The Rise, Fall, and Enduring Mystique of New England's (Second) Greatest NHL Franchise* (New York: Lyons Press, 2021), 163.

6. Thomas Aiello, *Dixieball: Race and Professional Basketball in the Deep South, 1947-1979* (Knoxville: University of Tennessee Press, 2021), 60–61.

7. Clayton Trutor, *Loserville: How Professional Sports Remade Atlanta—and How Atlanta Remade Professional Sports* (Lincoln: University of Nebraska, 2001), xiii–xv.

8. James C. Cobb, *Away Down South: A History of Southern Identity* (Oxford: Oxford University Press, 2005), 234.

9. *Fort Lauderdale News and Sun-Sentinel*, February 18, 1967, 16A.

10. Louis D. Rubin Jr., "The American South: The Continuity of Self-Definition," in *The American South: Portrait of a Culture*, ed. Louis D. Rubin, Jr. (Washington, DC: United States Information Agency, 1979), 6.

11. Melissa Carroll, "How Canada Became a Player in the 1960s," *CBC*, June 12, 2018, Web.

12. R. Ben Fawcett and Ryan Walker, "Indigenous Peoples, Indigenous Cities," in *Canadian Cities in Transition,* ed. Markus Moos, Tara Vinodrai, and Ryan Walker (Oxford University Press, 2020), 54.

13. Todd McCallum, *Hobohemia and the Crucifixion Machine: Rival Images of a New World in 1930s' Vancouver* (Edmonton: *Athabasca University*, 2014), 8–10.

14. Jack Richards, "Sandlotters Need Backing," *The Vancouver Sun,* December 19, 1952, 21.

15. A. W. Moscarella, "Let's Go, Vancouver," *The Province,* December 12, 1952, 4.

16. Erwin Swangard, "Follow the Sun," *The Vancouver Sun*, January 17, 1953, 16.

17. Jason Beck," Erwin Swangard," *BC Sports Hall of Fame,* Web

18. "Letters to the Editor," *The Vancouver Sun*, June 12, 1953, 4.

19. Peter S. Li, *The Chinese in Canada* (Oxford: Oxford University Press, 1988), 86.

20. Ibid., 93.

21. Alf Cottrell, "'Lions' New Moniker of B.C.'s WIFU Entry," *The Province,* April 2, 1953, 12.

22. Scott Simon, *Jackie Robinson and the Integration of Baseball* (New York: John Wiley & Sons, Inc., 2002), 98.

23. Frank P. Jozsa, Jr., *Major League Baseball Expansions and Relocations: A History, 1876-2008* (Jefferson, NC: McFarland, 2009), 47.

24. Ibid., 78–79.

25. Sportsnet Staff, "Raps Use Leaf Colours in Retro Huskies Jerseys," *SportsNet,* December 7, 2009, Web.

26. CBC Radio, "Before They Were the Raptors, Toronto's NBA Team was Nearly the Beavers, Hogs or Dragons," *CBC,* May 31, 2019, Web.

27. To be precise, they won one BAA and two NBA Championships.

28. Zach Scola and Brian S. Gordon, "A Conceptual Framework for Retro Marketing in Sport," *Sport Marketing Quarterly,* 2018, 27, 197–210.

29. Alan Goldstein, "IBA to Feature Short Talent, but League has Tall Ambitions," *The Baltimore Sun,* December 9, 1987, 5E.

30. Jim Taylor, "Another Slow Day on Sports Keyboard," *The Province,* December 10, 1987, 91.

31. "It's Only Four Years Away," *The Tacoma News Tribune,* January 3, 1982, 7.

32. Rod Ziegler, "It Wasn't Exactly Love at First Site . . . ," *Edmonton Journal,* August 4, 1984, 17.

33. Tony Gallagher, "Hoop Sold Short?," *The Province,* March 21, 1988, 18.

34. Mike Beamish, "Hawks Floored by Deal," *The Vancouver Sun,* April 29, 1988, E5.

35. Elliott Pap, "IBA Executives Say 'Don't Play," *The Vancouver Sun,* March 22, 1988, E1.

36. Dan Stinson, "Growing Pains Still Felt by New Basketball League," *The Vancouver Sun,* April 12, 1988, D8.

37. Leroy Byrd, "Just Watch Us," *The Province,* May 22, 1988, 82.

38. Jim Jamieson, "Hawks Wing It," *The Province,* July 8, 1988, 44.

39. Jim Jamieson, "It Was Mad Max in Management," *The Province,* September 8, 1988, 82.

40. "Curtain Falling on Basketball Nighthawks?," *The Vancouver Sun,* January 5, 1989, D1.

41. Mike Fleming, "Basketball League Offers Top Position to Memphis Man," *The Commercial Appeal,* March 26, 1988, D1.

42. Jim Jamieson, "WBL on a Rebound," *The Province,* March 5, 1989, 92.

43. Jim Jamieson, "Kodiak Arrest," *The Province,* March 22, 1989, 38.

Chapter 2

1. David DuPree, "NBA: Red Ink and a Bleak Future," *The Washington Post,* March 15, 1983, Web.

2. Chris Cobbs, "Widespread Cocaine Use by Players Alarms NBA," *The Washington Post,* August 20, 1980, Web.

3. Bob Sakamoto, "Cocaine—Scourge of the NBA," *Chicago Tribune,* February 16, 1986, Web.

4. John E. Merriam, "National Media Coverage of Drug Issues, 1983–1987," in *Communication Campaigns about Drugs: Government, Media, and the Public,* ed. Pamela J. Shoemaker (London: Routledge, 2009), 21.

5. Bob McComas, "Florida Cities in Running for NBA Team," *The Bradenton Herald,* January 9, 1987, D1.

6. Bill Jauss, "Eastern Illinois Center Finds Joy in 2d Round," *Chicago Tribune,* June 18, 1986, 4/2.

7. Joshua Mendelsohn, *The Cap: How Larry Fleisher and David Stern Built the Modern NBA* (Lincoln: University of Nebraska Press, 2020), 124.

8. Jamie Wayne, "Strauss Willing to Take Long Shot on Basketball," *National Post,* December 4, 1982, 11.

9. Joe Robbins, "CBA Playoffs: 8 of 10 Qualified," *Democrat and Chronicle,* November 13, 1980, 5D.

10. Jamie Wayne, "League is Trying to Net Canadian Basketball Team," *National Post,* January 7, 1984, 39.

11. Chris Baket, "$32.5-Million Price Tag Doesn't Scare Off Prospective Buyers," *Los Angeles Times,* April 19, 1987, Web.

12. Hal Brands, *From Berlin to Baghdad: America's Search for Purpose in the Post-Cold War World* (Lexington: The University Press of Kentucky, 2008), 98.

13. Ken Krause, "NBA Considering Cities in Canada," *The Akron Beacon Journal,* April 28, 1993, 26.

14. Associated Press, "Stern Says Teams Secure," *The Commercial Appeal,* February 10, 1996, D3.

15. Carson Cunningham. *American Hoops: U.S. Men's Olympic Basketball from Berlin to Beijing* (Lincoln: University of Nebraska Press), 347.

16. Chris McCosk, "Stern Measures Help NBA Flourish Globally," *Detroit Free Press,* October 25, 1995, 13D.

17. David Moore, "Challenges Await the NBA as It Goes Global in the '90s," *St. Louis Post-Dispatch,* November 15, 1992, 64.

18. Doug Ward, "Dazzling Addition to Skyline," *The Vancouver Sun,* September 21, 2005, E1

19. Mark Hume and David Baines, "The House That Arthur Built," *The Vancouver Sun*, November 16, 1996, A4.

20. Iain MacIntyre, "Vancouver Expansion Bid Made," *The Vancouver Sun*, April 15, 1993, C13.

21. Mike Beamish, "One-Team NBA Expansion Favors Toronto," *The Vancouver Sun*, April 28, 1993, D9.

22. Bill Barnard, "Toronto the Front-Runner in the NBA's Great White North Expansion," *Centre Daily Times*, September 21, 1993, D1.

23. Francine Dube, "Sports Glamour Lures Teens to Gamble," *Times Colonist*, January 27, 1994, C2.

24. Gary Kingston, "Name Naysayers Give Mounties Valuable Publicity," *The Vancouver Sun*, February 18, 1994, D6.

25. Paul Chapman, "Search on For a Name," *The Province*, April 29, 1994, A50.

26. Iain McIntyre, "Fur Will Fly," *The Vancouver Sun*, August 12, 1994, C1.

27. Jason Beck, "Gridiron 'Grizzlies' Came Way Before NBA Variety," *Vancouver is Awesome*, December 7, 2011, Web.

28. McIntyre, "Fur Will Fly," C1.

29. Howard Tsumura, "Jackson Lands in Dream Home," *The Province*, July 24, 1994, A69.

30. Associated Press, "Grizzlies Hire Winters," *The Clarksdale Press Register*, June 20, 1995, 7.

31. Ira Berkow," How Creighton's Dreams Came Apart," *The New York Times*, May 19, 1985, Web.

32. Chris Baker, "Growing Pains," *Los Angeles Times*, September 16, 1987, Web.

33. Howard Tsumura, "Blazers Bow to Big Ben," *The Province*, November 5, 1995, 81.

34. Paul Knepper, *The Knicks of the Nineties: Ewing, Oakley, Starks and the Brawlers That Almost Won It All* (Jefferson, NC: McFarland, 2020), 33.

35. Gary Kingston, "Grin and Bear It," *The Vancouver Sun*, June 26, 1995, D6.

36. Gary Kingston, "Grizzlies Know that Scoring Won't Be Automatic," *Calgary Herald*, October 14, 1995, D4.

37. Gary Kingston, "Grizzlies to Fans: Patience, Please," *The Vancouver Sun*, November 2, 1995, D2.

38. Kingston, "Grizzlies to Fans," D1.

39. Howard Tsumura, "Anthony Flips for Old Jersey Number," *The Province*, September 24, 1995, 68.

40. Steve Rushin, "Home on the Range," *Sports Illustrated*, November 29, 1993, 44–46.

41. Grant Kerr, "Big Country Comes to B.C," *The Whitehorse Star*, June 29, 1995, 18.

42. Jonathan Abrams, *Boys Among Men: How the Prep-to-Pro Generation Redefined the NBA and Sparked a Basketball Revolution* (New York: Crown Archetype, 2016), 31.

43. Dan Stinson and Gary Kingston, "With Benjamin Gone, Eyes Turn to Big Country," *The Vancouver Sun*, November 28, 1995, D11.

44. Howard Tsumura, "Expansion Nothing New for Former Hornet," *The Province*, October 12, 1995, A62.

45. Ronald Tillery, "Happy Anniversary," *The Commercial Appeal*, November 3, 2004, G8.

Chapter 3

1. Cleve Dheensaw, "Nash Express Follows NBA Star to Seattle," *Times Colonist*, March 15, 2003, B5.

2. Dave Feschuk and Michael Grange, *Steve Nash: The Unlikely Ascent of a Superstar* (Toronto: Vintage Canada, 2013), 40.

3. Ibid., 62.

4. Gary Kingston, "Grizzlies Grab Bibby," *The Vancouver Sun*, June 25, 1998, F1.

5. Emilie Quesnel, "Original Toronto Raptor Tracy Murray on How Team Became So Important to Canada," *CBC Radio*, May 20, 2019, Web.

6. Serena Kataoka, "Vancouverism: Actualizing the Livable City Paradox," *Berkeley Planning Journal* 22 (2009): 42.

7. Jeremy Sandler, "Cute or Sporty: The Making of a Mascot," *The Vancouver Sun*, June 11, 2001, B3.

8. Mike Baldwin, "Country Coming Home to Gans," *The Daily Oklahoman*, March 25, 2001, 14-B.

9. Brad Ziemer, "Big Country Scores Hit in Second Game," *The Vancouver Sun*, August 19, 1997, F4.

10. Kent Gilchrist, "Grizz, Raptors Different Beasts," *The Province*, February 26, 1996, A33.

11. John McKeachie, "Like Fries with That, Sir?," *The Province*, July 9, 1997, A49.

12. Thomas Golianopoulos, "'It Was All About Money': An Oral History of the 1998-99 NBA Lockout," *The Ringer*, February 14, 2019, Web.

13. Brad Ziemer, "Country Insists He's Ready to Play," *The Vancouver Sun,* January 13, 1999, F3.

14. Howard Tsumura, "Small Lifetime Ago," *The Province,* January 13, 1999, A44.

15. Gary Kingston, "Coach Shouts, Reeves Lapped as Camp Opens," *The Vancouver Sun,* January 23, 1999, D11c

16. Gary Mason, "Big Country's Battle of the Bulge," *The Vancouver Sun,* February 6, 1999, E1c.

17. Jim Morris, "Goodbye Grizzlies," *The Vancouver Sun,* April 14, 2001, G9.

18. Kerry Eggers, *Jail Blazers: How the Portland Trail Blazers Became the Bad Boys of Basketball* (New York: Sports Publishing, 2018), 243.

19. Ibid.

20. Frank Isola, "Play's Not the Thing," *Daily News,* June 30, 2007, 53.

21. Howard Beck, "Thomas's Deals Have Made the Knicks More Interesting," *The New York Times,* December 21, 2004, Web.

22. Ken Berger, "Eddy Needs Help to Reach Greatness," *Newsday,* February 21, 2007, A55.

23. Alan Hahn, "Isiah on Zach's 1-Game Ban: 'No Sweat,'" *Newsday,* January 5, 2008, A27.

24. Alan Hahn, "Steph: My Heart is Still Here," *Newsday,* March 6, 2008, A66.

25. Mark Heisler, "The Second Half," *The Los Angeles Times,* November 23, 2008, D6.

26. Ronald Tillery, "Iverson Heading out," *The Commercial Appeal,* November 17, 2009, A2.

27. Ronald Tillery, "Something to Prove," *The Commercial Appeal,* September 29, 2009, D1.

28. Ronald Tillery, "Randolph: My Image Tarnished," *The Commercial Appeal,* May 28, 2010, C2.

29. Ron Higgins, "City Loves Blue-Collar Attitude in Grizzlies' Playoff Run," *The Commercial Appeal,* May 15, 2011, D3.

30. "Grizzlies Hold on, Win Series 4-2 to Stun Top-Seeded Spurs," *Associated Press,* April 30, 2011.

31. Sam Anderson, *Boom Town: The Fantastical Saga of Oklahoma City, Its Chaotic Founding, Its Apocalyptic Weather, Its Purloined Basketball Team, and the Dream of Becoming a World-Class Metropolis* (New York: Crown, 2018), 43–44.

32. Nick Gunter, "Breakdown: A Look Back at Mississippi River Flood of May 2011," *Action5 News,* May 10, 2019, Web.

33. Adrian Saiz and Cain Burdeau, "Flood Threat Builds in Memphis," *The Arizona Republic*, May 7, 2011, A9.

34. David Schaper, "Memphis Landmarks Spared from River Flooding," *NPR*, May 9, 2011, Web.

35. "Grizzlies and American Red Cross to Assist Flood Victims," *NBA.com*, May 6, 2011, Web.

36. Higgins, "City Loves Blue-Collar Attitude."

37. Marlon W. Morgan, "Grizzlies Charity Honored," *The Commercial Appeal*, July 15, 2011, D1.

38. Chris Peck, "Lockout Could be a Vibe Killer," *The Commercial Appeal*, July 2, 2011, A8.

39. Tzwi Twersky, "NBA Player Zach Randolph is Thinking About Starting a Record Label," *XXL*, January 16, 2015, Web.

Chapter 4

1. Steve Francis, "I Got a Story to Tell," *The Players' Tribune*, March 8, 2018, Web.

2. Ibid.

3. Ronald Tillery, "Francis Ready to Tutor Young Grizzlies," *The Commercial Appeal*, January 4, 2009, D5.

4. Howard Tsumura, "Bull Market Beats Bears," *The Province*, May 23, 1999, A76.

5. Antonio Daniels, "Training Camp Diary," *The Vancouver Sun*, October 3, 1997, D4.

6. Howard Tsumura, "Lynch, Rogers Thrive off the Bench," *The Province*, October 5, 1997, A78.

7. Mike Beamish, "Former Grizzlie Rogers Gets to Live His Dream as a Celtic," *The Vancouver Sun*, November 1, 1997, F4.

8. Howard Tsumura, "Grizz Will Have to Go to Francis," *The Province*, June 17, 1999, A80.

9. Howard Tsumura, "Odom-eter Reads up on Grizz," *The Province*, June 6, 1999, A83.

10. Dave Feschuk, "Newest Grizzly Not Happiest Bear in Camp," *National Post*, July 1, 1999, B14.

11. Ken Rosenthal, "Being No. 2 a No. 1 Pain for Francis," *The Baltimore Sun*, July 1, 1999, C1.

12. Dan Barnes, "Grizz-Rapts Game Just Exhibition," *Edmonton Journal,* August 17, 1999, D1.

13. Gordon McIntyre, "Jackson Frustrated," *The Province,* August 26, 1999, A62.

14. Gary Mason, "Grizzlies, Francis a Bad Combination," *The Vancouver Sun,* August 26, 1999, D1.

15. Mike Downey, "When Will They See the Light in the Piazza?," *The Los Angeles Times,* August 2, 1989, 5.

16. Tony Kornheiser, "Ferry Beats Clipper Trap, Fast Breaks to Rome," *The Olympian,* August 3, 1989, 4D.

17. Tom Sorensen, "Clippers Make It Tough to Keep a Straight Face," *The Charlotte Observer,* August 2, 1989, 1C.

18. Gary Mason, "Grizzlies Finally Do the Right Thing – Trade Francis," *The Vancouver Sun,* August 27, 1999, E1.

19. Mason, "Grizzlies, Francis a Bad Combination," D3.

20. Tony Gallagher, "Come Back When You Grow up, Kid," *The Star-Phoenix,* July 3, 1999, B4.

21. Jeffrey Lane, *Under the Boards: The Cultural Revolution in Basketball* (Lincoln: University of Nebraska Press, 2007), 40.

22. Geoff Calkins, "Lost in Transition," *The Commercial Appeal,* December 14, 2006, D2.

23. Chris Gaines, "The Complete History of Allen Iverson's Three-Game Career with the Memphis Grizzlies," *Complex,* September 9, 2016. Web.

24. Scott Cacciola, "Iverson Deal Born of Desperation," *The Commercial Appeal,* September 27, 2009, D2.

25. Ibid., D1.

26. Kent Babb, *Not a Game: The Incredible Rise and Unthinkable Fall of Allen Iverson* (New York: Atria Books, 2015), 265–66.

27. Scott Cacciola, "The Answer to What?," *The Commercial Appeal,* December 26, 2009, B6.

28. Associated Press, "Olajuwon Hints at Vancouver Move," *The Commercial Appeal,* June 5, 1995, D2.

29. Ronald Tilley, "Players, Management Believe A.I. Can Teach Young Grizzlies," *The Commercial Appeal,* September 10, 2009, C2.

Chapter 5

1. Scott Howard-Cooper, "Divac is Stirring Up Hornet's Nest With Retirement Threat," *The Los Angeles Times,* June 28, 1996, C1.

2. Chris Poynter and Brian Bennett, "Fans Flee Once-Beloved Team," *The Courier-Journal,* September 30, 2001, A8.

3. Leonard Laye, "Cowens Resigns as Hornets Coach," *The Charlotte Observer,* March 8, 1999, 5D.

4. James Jones, "New Orleans Hornets?," *Sun Herald,* January 11, 2002, C-1.

5. Keith B. Wood, *Memphis Hoops: Race and Basketball in the Bluff City, 1968-1997* (Knoxville: The University of Tennessee Press, 2021), 47.

6. Joe Biddle, "Grizzlies Open Amid Relief in Memphis," *The Tennessean,* November 2, 2001, 9C.

7. Wood, *Memphis Hoops,* 30.

8. Lewis Little, "New York Celtic-Pep Game One of Season's Features," *Nashville Banner,* January 30, 1927, 1.

9. Murry R. Nelson, *The National Basketball League: A History, 1935-1949* (Jefferson, NC: McFarland, 2009), 99

10. Wood, *Memphis Hoops,* 5.

11. Terry Pluto, *Loose Balls: The Short, Wild Life of the American Basketball Association* (New York: Simon & Schuster, 1990), 39.

12. Ibid., 64.

13. Wood, *Memphis Hoops,* 58.

14. Ibid., 62.

15. Woodrow Paige Jr., "The Pros Welcome the Decision to Merge," *The Commercial Appeal,* May 8, 1971, 25.

16. Ibid., 25.

17. Wood, *Memphis Hoops,* 64.

18. Ibid.

19. Pluto, *Loose Balls,* 244.

20. Scott Dodd and Tim Whitmire, "Value of Hornets Hitting Ticket Goals is Debated," *The Charlotte Observer,* March 15, 2002, 2B.

21. Gary Kingston, "Grizzlies New Owner Not Worried About Price," *The Vancouver Sun,* March 4, 2000, F4.

22. The Canadian Press, "Basketball Love Affair Turns Sour," *Times Colonist,* February 14, 2001, B5

23. Gary Kingston, "Grizzlies' Ownership Approval Slows to a Snail's Pace," *The Vancouver Sun,* March 2, 2000, F3.

24. Gary Kingston, "Grizzlies' Profile an Issue," *The Vancouver Sun*, January 28, 1999, D4.

25. Gary Kingston, "Players Amazed at Ownership 'Circus' and 'Hypocrisy,'" *The Vancouver Sun*, April 12, 2000, E3.

26. Gary Kingston, "Daly Turns Down Grizzlies' Offer," *The Vancouver Sun*, April 6, 2000, F5.

27. Jim Morris, "Orca Bay Seeking Partner," *Calgary Herald*, August 24, 1999, C2.

28. Tony Gallagher, "Grizzlies Fans Feel Betrayed," *St. Louis Post-Dispatch*, September 24, 1999, D7.

29. Bernie Miklasz, "Laurie Collects Sport Teams," *The Vancouver Sun*, September 24, 1999, E3.

30. Louis Graham, "Heisley's an Extrovert Yearning for Obscurity," *The Commercial Appeal*, May 27, 2001, A10.

31. Gary Mason, "Grizzlies Sold, Again," *The Vancouver Sun*, January 25, 2000, E2.

32. David Perlmutt, "Hard Work Has Paid for Grizzlies Owner," *The Charlotte Observer*, March 28, 2001, 7A.

33. Gary Kingston, "Heisley Considers 'Bailing out,'" *The Vancouver Sun*, January 13, 2001, B10.

34. Jim Morris, "Grizzlies' Owner, Stern to Meet," *Calgary Herald*, February 4, 2001, B6.

35. Chris Duncan, "Stadium Part of Lure for Grizzlies," *The Paducah Sun*, March 16, 2001, 1B.

36. Gary Kingston, "Heisley Not Concerned about Charlotte Bid," *The Vancouver Sun*, April 5, 2001, D3.

37. Mike McGraw, "A Move Heisley Had to Make," *The Daily Herald*, December 27, 2001, 2/3.

38. Ron Higgins, "Building a Better Bear," *The Commercial Appeal*, April 15, 2001, D5.

39. Ibid.

Chapter 6

1. Chris Peck, "Grizzlies Need Energetic Owners," *The Commercial Appeal*, December 27, 2006, A12.

2. David Williams, "FedEx Aggressively Woos NBA Grizzlies, Wants Rights to Name Team, New Arena," *The Commercial Appeal*, March 21, 2001, A1.

3. Richard Thompson, "FedEx Ready to Court Another Sport," *The Commercial Appeal*, March 21, 2001, A8.

4. David Williams, "Grizzlies Owner Returns, Deals with 'Pursuit Team,'" *The Commercial Appeal*, March 23, 2001, A2.

5. Richard Thompson, "NBA Quest Has a Noble Dimension," *The Commercial Appeal*, June 29, 2001, 5.

6. David Williams, "Secret Pursuit, Two Came Calling," *The Commercial Appeal*, October 7, 2001, 23.

7. Joe Biddle, "Calipari Memphis-bound?," *The Tennessean*, March 1, 2000, 2C.

8. Ivan Carter, "Calipari Struggling at Memphis," *The Kansas City Star*, December 30, 2000, D4.

9. Wayne Risher, "1st Tennessee Lights Get Pyramid Spirit," *The Commercial Appeal*, September 12, 1989, A4.

10. Lynn Zinser, "Pyramid Alters MSU's Horizon," *The Commercial Appeal*, June 10, 1991, D2.

11. Jimmie Covington, "Landmark Day," *The Commercial Appeal*, November 9, 1991, A10.

12. Louis Graham, "Pyramid Dreams, Pyramid Schemes," *The Commercial Appeal*, October 18, 1992, B2.

13. Louis Graham, "He Made Fast Sale; Now Can Shlenker Deliver the Goods?," *The Commercial Appeal*, January 13, 1991, A10.

14. Bill Haltom, "Shlenker-Pyramid is New Version of Old Story," *The Commercial Appeal*, July 6, 1991, A11.

15. Bill Dries, "History Upgrade," *Memphis Daily News*, April 20, 2018, Web.

16. Graham, "Pyramid Dreams," B6.

17. Jimmie Covington, "A Decade of Indecision and Delays Later, Arena Opens," *The Commercial Appeal*, November 10, 1991, A17.

18. Charles Bernsen, "Balancing Black Hopes, White Feats Will be Hard," *The Commercial Appeal*, October 5, 1991, A1.

19. David Kushma, "Look Again at the Pointed House," *The Commercial Appeal*, April 14, 2001, A10.

20. David Williams, "NBA Brass to Visit City Next Week," *The Commercial Appeal*, May 22, 2001, A2.

21. McGraw, "A Move Heisley Had to Make," 2/3

22. Blake Fontenay, "Arena Finance Plan Includes Several Sources," *The Commercial Appeal*, June 29, 2001, 3.

23. David Williams, "Opposition Threatened to Derail Arena," *The Commercial Appeal*, October 9, 2001, A9.

24. Ronald Tillery, "Grizzlies Have Wright Stuff in Former Tiger Star," *The Commercial Appeal*, October 14, 2001, D8.

25. Sean Devey, "Now is No Time for Webber to Leave Kings," *The Californian*, July 5, 2001, 5D.

26. David Williams, "Arena to Be Beacon for Memphis," *The Commercial Appeal*, June 29, 2001, 3.

27. Blake Fontenay, "Arena Groundbreaking Marks a New Beginning for Memphis," *The Commercial Appeal*, June 21, 2002, B2.

28. Zack McMillin, "Tigers Like New Player in Town," *The Commercial Appeal*, May 1, 2002, D6.

29. Jeremy Peppas, "Grizzlies Open Training Camp Today in Memphis," *The Jackson Sun*, October 1, 2002, 1B.

30. Tom Enlund, "School Time for Grizzlies," *The Sacramento Bee*, November 17, 2002, C5.

31. Woody Baird, "Hubieball Takes off in Memphis," *The Missoulian*, March 29, 2004, D3.

32. David Williams, "Arena Reaches Minority-Hiring Goals," *The Commercial Appeal*, August 20, 2004, C1.

33. David Williams, "Tigers to Prowl at Forum," *The Commercial Appeal*, February 10, 2004, A2.

34. Woody Baird, "New Memphis Arena Ready for Business," *The Jackson Sun*, September 6, 2004, 2B.

35. Colin Fly, "Grizzlies' Brown Retires," *The Desert Sun*, November 26, 2004, C4.

36. Geoff Calkins, "Hopes of Trade Aside, Stability Has Its Upside," *The Commercial Appeal*, October 5, 2004, C1.

37. Ronald Tillery, "Fratello Gets What Brown Deserved," *The Commercial Appeal*, August 7, 2005, C5.

38. Ibid.

39. Teresa M. Walker, "Clock Runs out on Jerry West with Grizzlies," *Journal Gazette*, April 18, 2007, C8.

Chapter 7

1. Sam Smith, "Memphis in a Grisly State," *Chicago Tribune*, May 8, 2006, 4/2.

2. David Williams, "Davis Remains a Team Player," *The Commercial Appeal*, October 8, 2006, A4.

3. Teresa M. Walker, "Grizzlies Owner Expect No Sale," *The Knoxville News-Sentinel*, December 21, 2006, D6.

4. Eric D. Williams, "Past, Present and Future," *The News Tribune*, October 28, 2008, C5.

5. Sam Smith, "Big Names Keep Bags Packed," *Chicago Tribune*, February 19, 2007, 4/2.

6. SI Staff, "Gasol Trade Sparks War of Words," *Sports Illustrated*, February 8, 2008, web.

7. Ronald Tillery, "Heisley's 'the Guy Making Decisions,'" *The Commercial Appeal*, February 3, 2008, D2.

8. Chris Sheridan, "What Were the Grizzlies Thinking? The GM Explains," *ESPN*, January 17, 2008, web.

9. Associated Press, "Grizzlies Pick UCLA's Love in First Round," *The Tennessean*, June 27, 2008, C3.

10. Sam Smith, "Strickland Doesn't Miss Point," *Chicago Tribune*, December 17, 2007, 4/2.

11. Wanda Rushing, *Memphis and the Paradox of Place: Globalization in the American South* (Chapel Hill: University of North Carolina Press, 2009), 117.

12. Greg Jayne, "A Glimpse into the Future of the Blazers," *The Columbian*, April 15, 2007, B8.

13. Bob Young, "Suns Job Challenge to Hollins," *The Arizona Republic*, June 21, 1988, C5.

14. Ronald Tillery, "Former Griz Aide Couldn't Resist," *The Commercial Appeal*, November 14, 2008, D4.

15. Scott Cacciola, "A Shot at the Top," *The Commercial Appeal*, January 30, 2009, D3.

16. Adam Kilgore, "Elite Backcourt Brought on Board," *The Boston Globe*, June 25, 2004, E8.

17. Marc Stein, "Deal for Memphis Grizzlies Reached," *ESPN*, June 11, 2012, Web.

18. Ronald Tillery, "Griz Players, Coaches Ready to Meet Pera," *The Commercial Appeal*, October 26, 2012, 3D.

19. J. J. Adams, "NBA Pre-Season Match Turns into Grizzlies Love-in," *The Vancouver Sun*, October 18, 2019, C11.

Conclusion

1. Andrei S. Markovits and Lars Renmann, *Gaming the World: How Sports Are Reshaping Global Politics and Culture* (Princeton, NJ: Princeton University Press, 2010), 11.

2. Rushing, *Memphis and the Paradox of Place*, 145.

3. Mark Giannotto, "Morant's Secret Weapon is His Family," *The Commercial Appeal*, February 23, 2020, A1.

4. Giannotto, A12.

5. Mark Giannotto, "Ja Morant's Brand is Reaching New Highs. What Might That Be Worth to Memphis?" *The Commercial Appeal*, January 20, 2022. Web.

Bibliography

Books

Abrams, Jonathan. *Boys Among Men: How the Prep-to-Pro Generation Redefined the NBA and Sparked a Basketball Revolution*. New York: Crown Archetype, 2016.

Aiello, Thomas. *Dixieball: Race and Professional Basketball in the Deep South, 1947–1979*. Knoxville: University of Tennessee Press, 2021.

Anderson, Sam. *Boom Town: The Fantastical Saga of Oklahoma City, Its Chaotic Founding, Its Apocalyptic Weather, Its Purloined Basketball Team, and the Dream of Becoming a World-Class Metropolis*. New York: Crown, 2018.

Babb, Kent. *Not a Game: The Incredible Rise and Unthinkable Fall of Allen Iverson*. New York: Atria Books, 2015.

Baumann, Zygmunt. *Liquid Modernity*. Cambridge, UK: Polity, 2000.

Berelowitz, Lance. *Dream City: Vancouver and the Global Imagination*. Vancouver: Douglas & McIntyre, 2005.

Brands, Hal. *From Berlin to Baghdad: America's Search for Purpose in the Post-Cold War World*. Lexington: The University Press of Kentucky, 2008.

Cobb, James C. *Away Down South: A History of Southern Identity*. Oxford: Oxford University Press, 2005.

Colas, Yago. *Ball Don't Lie!: Myth, Genealogy, and Invention in the Cultures of Basketball*. Philadelphia, PA: Temple University Press, 2016.

Cunningham, Carson. *American Hoops: U.S. Men's Olympic Basketball from Berlin to Beijing*. Lincoln: University of Nebraska Press, 2010.

Eggers, Kerry. *Jail Blazers: How the Portland Trail Blazers Became the Bad Boys of Basketball*. New York: Sports Publishing, 2018.

Feschuk, Dave, and Michael Grange. *Steve Nash: The Unlikely Ascent of a Superstar*. Toronto: Vintage Canada, 2013.

Jozsa Jr., Frank P., *Major League Baseball Expansions and Relocations: A History, 1876–2008*. Jefferson, NC: McFarland, 2009.

Kennedy, Joe. *Games without Frontiers*. London: Repeater Books, 2016.

Knepper, Paul. *The Knicks of the Nineties: Ewing, Oakley, Starks and the Brawlers That Almost Won It All*. Jefferson, NC: McFarland, 2020.

Lane, Jeffrey. *Under the Boards: The Cultural Revolution in Basketball*. Lincoln: University of Nebraska Press, 2007.

Li, Peter S. *The Chinese in Canada*. Oxford: Oxford University Press, 1988.

Markovits, Andrei S., and Lars Renmann. *Gaming the World: How Sports Are Reshaping Global Politics and Culture*. Princeton, NJ: Princeton University Press, 2010.

McCallum, Todd. *Hobohemia and the Crucifixion Machine: Rival Images of a New World in 1930s' Vancouver*. Edmonton, CAN: *Athabasca University*, 2014.

Mendelsohn, Joshua. *The Cap: How Larry Fleisher and David Stern Built the Modern NBA*. Lincoln: University of Nebraska Press, 2020.

Naismith, James. *The James Naismith Reader: Basketball in His Own Words*, edited by Douglas Stark. Lincoln: University of Nebraska Press, 2021.

Nelson, Murry R. *The National Basketball League: A History, 1935–1949*. Jefferson, NC: McFarland, 2009.

Pickens, Pat. *The Whalers: The Rise, Fall, and Enduring Mystique of New England's (Second) Greatest NHL Franchise*. New York: Lyons Press, 2021.

Pluto, Terry. *Loose Balls: The Short, Wild Life of the American Basketball Association. New York:* Simon & Schuster, 1990.

Rushing, Wanda. *Memphis and the Paradox of Place: Globalization in the American South*. Chapel Hill: The University of North Carolina Press, 2009.

Simon, Scott. *Jackie Robinson and the Integration of Baseball*. New York: John Wiley & Sons, Inc., 2002.

Tarver, Erin C. *The I in Team: Sports Fandom and the Reproduction of Identity*. Chicago: The University of Chicago Press, 2017.

Trutor, Clayton. *Loserville: How Professional Sports Remade Atlanta—and How Atlanta Remade Professional Sports*. Lincoln: University of Nebraska, 2001.

Wood, Keith B. *Memphis Hoops: Race and Basketball in the Bluff City, 1968–1997. Knoxville:* The University of Tennessee Press, 2021.

Academic Articles and Chapters in Anthologies

Fawcett, R. Ben, and Ryan Walker. "Indigenous Peoples, Indigenous Cities." In *Canadian Cities in Transition,* edited by Markus Moos, Tara Vinodrai, and Ryan Walker, 51–69. Oxford: Oxford University Press, 2020.

Kataoka, Serena. "Vancouverism: Actualizing the Livable City Paradox." *Berkeley Planning Journal* 22, no. 1 (2009): 42–57.

Merriam, John E. "National Media Coverage of Drug Issues, 1983–1987." In *Communication Campaigns about Drugs: Government, Media, and the Public,* edited by Pamela J. Shoemaker, 21–29. London: Routledge, 2009.

Rubin, Louis D. Jr. "The American South: The Continuity of Self-Definition." In *The American South: Portrait of a Culture,* edited by Louis D. Rubin, Jr., 3–22. Washington, DC: United States Information Agency, 1979.

Schlesinger, Arthur Jr. "New Mood in Politics." In *The Sixties: Art, Politics, and Media of Our Most Explosive Decade,* edited by Gerald Howard, 44–55. St. Paul, MN: Paragon House, 1991.

Scola, Zach, and Brian S. Gordon. "A Conceptual Framework for Retro Marketing in Sport." *Sport Marketing Quarterly* 27 (2018): 197–210.

Swindell, David, and Mark S. Rosentraub. "Who Benefits from the Presence of Professional Sports Teams? The Implications for Funding of Stadiums and Arenas." *Public Administration Review* 58, no. 1 (Jan-Feb, 1998): 11–20.

Wells, Tom. "Running Battle: Washington's War at Home," in *Long Time Gone: Sixties America Then and Now,* edited by Alexander Bloom, 75–98. Oxford: Oxford University Press, 2001.

Newspapers and Magazines

The Akron Beacon Journal
The Arizona Republic
Associated Press
The Baltimore Sun
The Bradenton Herald
Calgary Herald
The Californian
Centre Daily Times
The Charlotte Observer
Chicago Tribune
The Clarksdale Press Register
The Columbian

The Commercial Appeal
The Courier-Journal
Daily News
The Daily Oklahoman
Democrat and Chronicle
The Desert Sun
Detroit Free Press
Edmonton Journal
Fort Lauderdale News and Sun-Sentinel
The Jackson Sun
Journal Gazette
The Kansas City Star

Los Angeles Times

The Missoulian

Nashville Banner

National Post

The New York Times

Newsday

The Olympian

The Paducah Sun

The Province

The Sacramento Bee

Sports Illustrated

St. Louis Post-Dispatch

The Star-Phoenix

Sun Herald

The Tacoma News Tribune

The Tennessean

Times Colonist

The Vancouver Sun

The Washington Post

The Whitehorse Star

Websites

Action5 News

BC Sports Hall of Fame

CBC

Complex

Memphis Daily News

NBA.com

NPR

The Players' Tribune

The Ringer

SportsNet

Vancouver is Awesome

XXL

Index

Page numbers in **boldface** refer to
illustrations.